Love, Healing and Happiness

Larry Culliford

By the same author (as Patrick Whiteside)

The Little Book of Happiness
The Little Book of Bliss
Happiness: The 30-Day Guide That Will Last You a Lifetime

Winchester, UK
Washington, USA)

First published by O Books, 2007
O Books is an imprint of John Hunt Publishing Ltd., The Bothy, Deershot Lodge,
Park Lane, Ropley, Hants, SO24 0BE, UK
office1@o-books.net
www.o-books.net

Distribution in:

UK and Europe
Orca Book Services
orders@orcabookservices.co.uk
Tel: 01202 665432 Fax: 01202 666219 Int. code (44)

USA and Canada
NBN
custserv@nbnbooks.com
Tel: 1 800 462 6420 Fax: 1 800 338 4550

Australia and New Zealand
Brumby Books
sales@brumbybooks.com
Tel: 61 3 9761 5535 Fax: 61 3 9761 7095

Far East (offices in Singapore, Thailand, Hong Kong, Taiwan)
Pansing Distribution Pte Ltd
kemal@pansing.com
Tel: 65 6319 9939 Fax: 65 6462 5761

South Africa
Alternative Books
altbook@peterhyde.co.za
Tel: 021 447 5300 Fax: 021 447 1430

Text copyright Larry Culliford 2007

Design: Stuart Davies

ISBN-13: 978 1 905047 91 8
ISBN-10: 1 905047 91 6

A CIP catalogue record for this book is available from the British Library.

Printed in the US by Maple Vail

Love, Healing and Happiness

Spiritual Wisdom for Secular Times

Larry Culliford

BOOKS

Winchester, UK
Washington, USA

MORE ENDORSEMENTS FOR
LOVE, HEALING AND HAPPINESS.

Larry Culliford is a born story-teller, and the stories told in this book capture the essence of what it is to be human; to be mentally and physically vulnerable and yet through the pain of adversity, to grow in wisdom and stature. As a psychiatrist with many years of clinical experience, he offers a unique and personal account of his life and work, showing how everyone has in their hands the key to their healing. This is a book of practical spirituality and one not to be missed. **Dr Andrew Powell**. Founding Chair of the "Spirituality and Psychiatry" Special Interest Group of the Royal College of Psychiatrists, London.

Dr. Larry Culliford's book, "Love, Healing and Happiness: Spiritual Wisdom for a Post-secular Era", is an unputdownable read. He is a marvellous writer, a born story-teller. His book is saying vitally important things about our need for a deep, spiritual life.

Influenced by Viktor Frankl's book, "Man's Search for Meaning", Culliford profoundly understands people's deep need to tell their stories, and he encourages his patients not only to narrate their unique stories but also to own them, because imbedded within them lies the very wisdom that helps them live their lives. An added boon is that Culliford practices his own counsel: he shares his own life story with his readers so that we're allowed a glimpse into his soul-journey, one fraught with shadow and light, challenge and mystery, a journey that is a search for a deeper, holy-holistic life through self-examination, through the study not only of Christianity but also of all the wisdom religions, including Zen Buddhism, Hinduism and

Taoism; thus, he can describe himself as a "universalist Christian", one who's also a church-going Anglican. In the tradition of Robert Coles' work of marrying psychology and story, this is a wisely "wholeminded" book, and readers will be spiritually refreshed if not transformed.

Robert Waldron. Long-term teacher of English Literature and Language at Boston Latin School, and prize-winning author of articles and books including, "Thomas Merton in Search of His Soul".

I was very impressed by Larry Culliford's new book. It is a remarkably comprehensive and intriguing guide to psychological and spiritual development, always clear, often moving and most relevant to our current cultural predicament. Along the way, Larry illustrates the practice of modern psychiatry at its best, inspired as it should be by spiritual as well as psychological and biological awareness. Many people will recognise aspects of themselves in the stories used to illuminate his vision of the spiritual path.

The style is easy, and carries the reader along in spite of the weight of the subject matter. I particularly appreciated the discussion about the drawbacks of democracy. The book will appeal to all those who have glimpsed the 'Wisdom Mind', and will enable them to recognise more vividly that aspect of the soul, thus fostering spiritual growth. I was struck once again by the similarities between the underlying message from all the great religions and wisdom traditions. I wish the book all success, and think it will attain that on its merits.

Dr. Julian Candy. Retired psychiatrist, Hampshire, UK.

In this renaissance of spirituality, Larry Culliford's personal and scholarly contribution – representing East and West, ancient and contemporary – is readable, reassuring, and reinvigorating. He offers not quite a recipe for spiritual health, but an explanation of how to grow beyond our everyday mind to our wisdom mind, which brings wholeness.

Sister Monica Weis SSJ, Professor of English, Nazareth College, Rochester NY, USA, and past vice president of the International Thomas Merton Society.

Larry Culliford has drawn together insights from his professional training and pastoral care interactions plus his own personal explorations and journey, and has woven the different threads together beautifully. It holds together most effectively and, as a result, has the possibility of touching on the thoughts, emotions and spiritual yearnings of those who read it.

Rev. Dr. Stuart Johnson. Anglican Priest and senior NHS Chaplain.

This is a book about spiritual and emotional well being – challenging and accessible for all who search for life's meaning. I think people will find it very helpful. Larry Culliford's storytelling is steeped in a wisdom inspired by psychological insight and spiritual traditions, yet grounded in real life and everyday experience.

Fiona Gardner. Psychotherapist and author; currently Chair of The Thomas Merton Society of Great Britain and Ireland.

There are many self-help books which will teach you techniques to make yourself happy. Dr. Larry Culliford, on the other hand, takes the trouble to explain the roots of happiness, opening up the possibility that we can *be* happy. It is partly about getting to grips with our place in the universe, and here Larry is not afraid to use the kind of spiritual language that is appropriate for what he calls a "post-secular" age. Above all, he knows what he is talking about. From his long experience as a psychiatrist, he talks about the kind of discoveries about oneself – and about the other – that can be truly healing.

Kenneth Wilson. Priest and Director of Soul of India Tours.

The book is very beautifully written, weaving together personal stories with both theory and practice. The short chapters make the book very readable, so that it does not need to be rushed as it requires reflection. Those at the end of each chapter are helpful in this. The universal approach will make the book very appealing to the less religious, but religious people will also benefit from its content, and I agree wholeheartedly that being able to take into serious and thoughtful account the beliefs and practices of other faiths can truly enhance our own. Larry describes a variety of stages of faith development that provide models for people to develop for themselves. I particularly valued the sections on *Conditioning and Conformity* and *Love, Sex and Maturity*. It is definitely a book to challenge and support people who are able to acknowledge and value the spiritual life on their spiritual journey.

Rev. Peter Wells. Senior Chaplain, Brighton and Sussex University Hospitals NHS Trust, UK.

Dr Larry Culliford trained in medicine at St. Catharine's College, Cambridge and Guy's Hospital, London. He works as a psychiatrist in Sussex, England. He teaches a course on spirituality and health care at the Brighton and Sussex Medical School. He has written several successful self-help books using the pen-name Patrick Whiteside (see: www.happinesssite.com). He was a co-founder of the Royal College of Psychiatrists 'Spirituality and Psychiatry' Special Interest Group (www.rcpsych.ac.uk/spirit). He is a member of the Thomas Merton Society of Great Britain and Ireland (www.thomasmertonsociety.org), the International Thomas Merton Society (www.merton.org) and the Scientific and Medical Network (www.scimednet.org).

Larry refers to himself as a universalist Christian. A churchgoing Anglican, he is open to the teachings and practices of many world faith traditions. He has studied with Buddhist teachers and has meditated regularly for over 20 years.

Dedication:

For the many friends and followers of Thomas Merton (1915-68)

Where there is questioning,
There is something beyond the question…
Those who dispute do not see.
From Chuang Tsu's *Inner Chapters*

This is Perfect.
That is Perfect.
Perfect comes from Perfect.

Take Perfect from Perfect
And the remainder is Perfect.
From Hindu Scripture

Whereof we cannot speak, thereat we may well be amazed!

Contents

Introduction

People are storytellers. Stories are important to us. They often make us feel happy when we hear or read them. By explaining things about which we are curious and possibly anxious, stories have the power to teach, calm and reassure us. Storytelling arouses a spirit of enquiry that entertains and educates us from childhood onwards. For all these reasons, this book contains several stories, most of them about real people (although I have changed the names).

Many of the tales, like those of Kelly, June, Veronica and Keith, have come from my professional practice, some are personal (such as the story about my Grandfather's final prophetic words), some came from dreams, and others are more like allegories or parables.

The stories told in this book introduce and develop a number of themes related to love, healing and happiness. The cover picture has been chosen carefully by way of illustration – the sun provides energy, warmth and light, and is necessary for life. It is essential to us. This great nearby star is always shining, whether we see it directly or not. At night, its light is reflected back to us by the moon. Often obscured by clouds, it nevertheless influences us all the time.

There is an allegorical story towards the end of the book about a man living in shadow who goes in search of sunlight. The sun is symbolic of a similarly essential and cosmic source of energy, of life, love and healing. This inexhaustible fountain also seems hidden from us but, like the sun, remains a constant influence for our benefit. The sacred wellspring has many names according to a wide range of spiritual traditions. We will explore the process of naming what is absolute and infinite and visit various tales told about our origins, to see how they might be reconciled. One of the main themes of this book is that we are connected to this source, this spirit, by our breath, and intimately through it to each other.

Another of the main themes is that we can be said to develop psychological and spiritual maturity through a series of six stages. Although humanity currently appears to be going through a kind of adolescent period, we will continue to mature by improving our capacity for a holistic or 'wholeminded' approach to life.

Wholeminded awareness, which we can learn from meditation practice, brings our wisdom minds into play, fostering universal interconnectedness. Over time, this naturally brings about the healing of emotional wounds and broken relationships. Mrs Cruikshank's remarkable story in chapter 12, for example, shows how we may continue growing as individuals, right to the end of life. We can hope to make progress collectively too, generation by generation, and learn eventually to avoid the high levels of hardship, conflict and related distress that currently exist in local, national and international communities. We can hope for general and widespread improvement in terms of happiness and contentment.

Many of the stories we tell each other, and listen to daily through the media, are of human suffering. Today's BBC news broadcast was typical, with accounts of climate change and famine threatening millions of lives, also of war, torture and terrorism. There were reports of child sexual abuse, of two murders (one involving a very young suspect), and of a multi-million pound robbery involving the brutal kidnap of a family. There was also a story about allegations of fraud and financial wrongdoing by those close to political leaders.

In these stories there seem to be common underlying themes of both greed and fear. At the heart of each distressing event, there is a clash between self-seeking, materialistic and secular values on the one hand and altruistic, universal and spiritual values on the other. Ambiguity and double standards are widespread. Uncertainty and ambivalence prevail. This is typical during adolescence, which is a time for discovering boundaries, for finding out what seems to work and what doesn't. For some, it means avoiding responsibility and finding out what you can get away with. This is all part of growing up, and not entirely avoidable; but there are many who want now to move on. Although we live in times domonated by secular thinking and values, the time is now ripe for renewal of the balance between the spiritual and the worldly.

Humanity's current 'adolescent' period seems to be both painful and prolonged. We have not yet learned about and accepted the value of suffering and its powers of transformation – the fact that pain can help us grow and mature.

In a secular society, such as emerged alongside immensely destructive wars and totalitarian dictatorships during the twentieth century, there is widespread denial of what is unseen, undetectable and scientifically unmeasurable. This leads to a dominance of worldly over spiritual values. The result is a potentially harmful neglect of spiritual knowledge, spiritual practices and spiritual skills.

Research and experience both show, however, that human spirituality can be suppressed but never extinguished. It finds expression, for example, in the almost but not quite sacred and iconic use of religious and spiritual motifs in popular culture and advertising. There is a celebrated singer, for example, who is called Madonna, the traditional name of respect for the Holy Mother of Christ. In another instance, a renowned footballer poses as the Risen Christ in Michael Browne's picture, "The Art of the Game", based very precisely on Pierro della Francesca's magnificent and inspiring fifteenth-century fresco, "The Resurrection".

Even when religious and spiritually related subjects are borrowed and sometimes amusingly lampooned, for example when actors dressed as priests portray devotion to a brand name beer, some deference towards their sacred origin is retained. The images yet speak to a profound yearning within us. The words 'jaguar' and 'rover', for example, used as names for cars, have all but lost their original meanings of big cat and a person who wanders the countryside. Nevertheless, the manufacturers and advertisers rely on these associations with the beauty and power of nature, with excitement and freedom of the spirit. It may be coincidence, but one slogan for a high-powered off-road vehicle – Go Beyond! – appears identical to the first words of *The Little Book of Bliss*, which I wrote promoting spiritual awareness. Language and images like these appeal to our most basic and primary needs. As we search for meaning and significance, they suggest that we are accepted and valued at the highest level, offering us a sublime sense of unity with a most glorious creation.

Although contemporary culture has a tendency to close down spiritual awareness, it cannot do so completely. Within secularism lie the seeds of its own transformation in the direction of spirituality. In the 1880s, the philosopher Friedrich Nietzsche famously declared 'God is dead'. The phrase has since become something of a slogan for secularists; but according to the Christian story, the crucified God rose again. After a period of mourning and confusion, the Resurrection took place and, according to St Paul, 'Christ once raised from the dead dies no more: death has no more dominion over him'. (Romans chapter 6, verse 9) Whether followers of the Christian tradition or not, we can try to respect and gain from this most powerful and hopeful story.

If we do not find holy inspiration, we may never emerge from adolescence. Victims of worldly success, we may perish as a people through the conflicts associated with competition for scarce natural resources and living space, and the pollutant effects of ungovernable consumerism.

The views presented in this book are that life and the spirit are irrepressible, and that we are capable of growing through suffering. Nietzsche's dictum can be resolved into this: "God is dead until God comes alive within us". That which is Divine and Holy can come alive within us because the Spirit, eternally alive, is accessible and available through the faculties of our wisdom minds.

As people mature, attachment to worldly, secular values naturally diminishes. Spiritual wisdom grows and matures spontaneously. Although no precise timetable can be forecast, a spiritual reawakening and the new dawn of a post-secular era can be predicted with confidence.

My intention in writing this book is to offer an opportunity for readers to reconsider a spiritual perspective on life, and to offer some guidance. Trying to influence the thoughts, feelings, beliefs and practices of others can lead rapidly to conflict; so progress is wisely pursued and easiest at the individual level. If it is difficult to influence others, even for their own good, we can at least seek love, healing and happiness for ourselves. This will, in any case, benefit those around us. A more precise description of a major theme of the book, then, is concerned with personal development, and about how personally to make the most of ill fortune. Collective development will follow.

My patients have taught me that everyone experiences a drive for meaning and a sense of purpose in life. Everyone wants to feel that, somewhere and somehow, they belong. We face loss and the threat of loss daily; but we can seek to grow through adversity instead of trying to avoid it. That nature is set up for us to do so is an aspect of the book's main theme. Emotional healing is a process leading naturally, through letting go of attachment and the accep-tance of loss, to the resolution and reversal of painful feelings. Anxiety is converted to calm. Sorrow gives way to joy. We grow through completion of the emotional healing process, finding reliable new levels of insight, equanimity and contentment.

A key element in maturing as individuals involves the discarding or dissolving of false masks, the results of early life conditioning. They are false mainly in the sense of being incomplete. We seek and hope eventually to discover, however gradually, our true and perfect selves; perfect not in the sense of flawless, but in the sense of whole. It is this aspect of wholeness that enables the wisdom mind, attuned constantly to the unity of the universe, to assist us.

Obscured in adolescence by the clouds of conditioning, of

everyday consciousness and our daily concerns, the wisdom mind shines on into our lives nevertheless, like the sun. As we engage in spiritual practices and develop spiritual skills, so will the mists thin and the clouds roll away. Meditation, a form of silent prayer requiring no special belief, is exceptionally helpful, both as a practice in itself and through enhancing the experience and effects of other spiritual practices. This kind of prayer is not about asking for what we need, but about creating an internal environment in which it is easier to recognize our deepest needs and so work towards and get what we really want. What we really want is happiness itself. The world's religions contain much spiritual wisdom, all of it available through scripture and useful whether you adhere to any particular faith tradition or none. That is why such wisdom is also sprinkled throughout this book.

About twenty-five years ago, I had a wonderful dream. I was in a grey, barren landscape of vast horizons under a dark sky. In my hand was some kind of prospecting implement, and over my shoulder a collecting sack. In the far distance there were just two or three isolated figures, heads bowed like mine, eyes down towards the ground. I was ambling beside a fast-flowing stream, one of several criss-crossing the rather muddy area. At first I felt lost, unsure of what I was doing or seeking. Soon, however, I noticed a small, beautiful, teardrop-shaped ingot of pure gold on the ground at my feet. The tool I held was well designed to dislodge it. Picking it up and placing it in my bag, I immediately noticed another small but perfect golden sculpture, then another. It was as if I could reap this treasure because I could see it where others could not. I knew then that most of them had lost interest in prospecting, and had gone away to enjoy themselves and have fun. I felt that I wanted to continue collecting this priceless golden jewellery, but I also wanted to share my secret with loved ones. As the dream ended, I was wondering whether to stay or go and look for others to tell them the news.

If the beautifully-shaped ingots represent nuggets of spiritual wisdom, I have been prospecting for them in the landscapes of medicine and psychiatry, of spirituality and religion, of world travel and contemporary life, ever since. I have always also wanted to share what I seem to have learned, at least to point others in its direction. I can only hope that the golden wisdom is genuine, and that my words measure up to the task of conveying at least a fraction of the amazing wealth available through opening ourselves wholemindedly to the great, sacred, mysterious and universal Source of love, healing and happiness. Only you, the reader, will know if it works for you. If this book helps even one person, I will consider it to be a success.

Larry Culliford
Sussex, Easter 2006.

1. The Wisdom Mind of Love

Kelly was born and raised in Sydney, Australia. I found myself in that city too, within a couple of years of completing medical training, working in general practice after hospital posts in medicine, surgery and psychiatry. At the time I was running a single-handed practice in a Sydney suburb while the regular doctor was on holiday. The practice was attractively situated, close to the famous harbour.

One warm, bright, sunny day I was feeling good to be alive when an attractive, young and apparently healthy woman came for the first consultation of the day. This was Kelly. She complained that she had been irritable for several days and now could not stop weeping. She was alarmed, thinking that she might be losing her mind.

I recall asking about her life and whether she could think of any particular problems that might be affecting her mood. She said there were none. Her childhood had been happy. She was part of a loving and supportive family. Her parents, brothers and sister were all living and well. She had a rewarding job and was earning sufficient money. She also had a loving boyfriend, Brett. She had many friends, an active social and sporting life, so she could think of nothing upsetting her life.

I can still picture the sunlit room, with this puzzled young woman sitting opposite me. Her arms were folded, and I happened to notice that she was stroking her right elbow rhythmically with her left hand. An idea occurred to me, and I asked Kelly to reflect a little longer on the possibility that she was experiencing some kind of loss. The room was still and silent while Kelly pondered.

Eventually, she looked up. "I don't think it's anything," she began. I waited. "I was pregnant a few months ago,' she continued, "but Brett and I decided that this was not the time to have a baby, so I went for a termination." I waited a little longer. "You don't think that could have anything to do with how I've been feeling, do you?" she asked, looking into my eyes once again.

"When exactly was that?" I replied. 'When would your baby have been born?'

Kelly thought for a second and seemed surprised by the answer. "About now", she said. She was still stroking her arm as if she were cradling a baby, so I gently drew her attention to that. I did not need to ask whether she now thought there might be a connection between the pregnancy and her emotions. Kelly grasped the point immediately.

"Oh, yes!" She was evidently a little shocked. "Deep down, now I think about it,' she said, "I really wanted that baby. It just wasn't the right time." Kelly was still unhappy, but pleased to have found the reason for her sorrow. At least she knew she wasn't losing her mind.

Kelly's wisdom mind at work

Kelly's irritability and sadness seemed to make sense. She had voluntarily given up, and so lost irretrievably, a part of herself: her first pregnancy. She was grieving for what might have been: the prospect of a child. Without knowing it, she had formed a powerful attachment with something this non-existent child still represented.

There was an unconscious bond of love with something created biologically within her body, but also psychologically within her imagination. Her spontaneous irritability and tears, synchronised with the due birthdate of her unborn baby, were telling her that she needed to pay attention to her feelings and adapt to what was a genuine and painful loss.

It may seem strange to say it, but our minds often seem to know more than we think. There is a distinction to be made between our *everyday* minds and what we can refer to as our *wisdom* minds – our wisdom minds are tuned permanently to the 'bigger picture'. Here is an example. It may have been my wisdom mind, my intuition, which prompted me to make the connection between Kelly's cradling gesture and her weeping. It was certainly her own wisdom mind which prompted both the deep-seated emotional reaction and her immediate understanding of its significance, once I pointed this out. This is why we can think of it as the wisdom mind. In a way that often seems mysterious, it both immediately and incontrovertibly knows best.

For Kelly, that moment of revelation and insight in the doctor's office enabled the completion of a natural emotional healing process regarding her loss. It had begun a few days earlier when her mood changed, but had been halted by her bewilderment. She was not only unhappy, she was also feeling confused about her painful feelings, which were unexpected. She was feeling bad about feeling bad.

Discovering a rational explanation for her sadness took care of Kelly's bewilderment and helped her feel good again about her pain. This in turn allowed the healing emotional process to continue to the point of resolution without further hindrance. Kelly left the office accepting the emotional consequences of her decision to arrange the termination of her pregnancy. I felt sure that she would not only recover fully, but also gain from the experience in both wisdom and maturity. This would be, for her, a valuable episode in terms of personal growth. She was learning about her own truest values, about what mattered most in her life.

I did not need to speak about this to Kelly at the time. I did not then understand it well enough myself to put it clearly into words. I simply recommended that she have a heart to heart talk with Brett, and reassured her that all would soon be well with her again, while offering another appointment if things did not seem to work out.

A week or so later, Kelly did come to see me again. She did not book but simply dropped in. The receptionist told me she seemed well and just wanted a quick word.

Kelly's plans for the future

Kelly was beaming when she came into my office the second time. "I'm fine, now,' she confirmed, "But I had to come back and thank you. I feel so much better. Brett and I have been talking. It turns out that he was feeling bad too, so we've decided to go ahead and start a family. We think we can afford it. We weren't sure before, but now it's what we both really want". "And," she added, "we are going to get married."

To give up the first pregnancy had, they both realised, been a genuine sacrifice, made with basically good motives, knowing that they were not yet ready to provide adequately, either materially or psychologically, for a child. To experience the consequent emotions of loss, followed by healing and reintegration, allowed Kelly to approach Brett for a meaningful discussion in a happier frame of mind about what they both really wanted. It prepared them for the future, and I remember thinking that they were likely to be better parents as a result of what had happened. Future children would benefit from the sacrifice of their older sibling.

Love, loss and the wisdom mind

When I was a student and newly qualified medical practitioner, I was involved in the delivery of about fifty babies, and each one seemed miraculous to me. I see childbirth as sacred; and it's no surprise to me that such powerful emotions can be involved when, as in Kelly's case, a pregnancy is terminated.

It seems best at this stage to reflect compassionately and set aside discussion of the moral and ethical issues involved; to avoid especially any temptation to be judgemental. Psychologically, concentrating especially on love and the emotional healing process, in Kelly's case the healing process allowed love to be a cure as well as the cause for her emotional pain and distress. She had fallen spontaneously in love with her pregnancy; but she did not recognise the strength of her attachment to it, and did not plan for the intensity of her reaction to losing it. Her tears surprised her, until we were able together to work out the explanation for them.

The wisdom mind seems lovingly to be in tune with the universe through being whole. This wholemindedness is the basis of its healing power. In this sense 'lovingly' also means seamlessly, without ambivalence, and so without hindrance. The great twentieth-century Swiss psychiatrist Jung[1] referred to this notion of wisdom mind as the 'collective unconscious'. It is a kind of mystery, and it may help to imagine it like this:

We use our *everyday* minds like laptop computers, carrying them around with us; but it is as if they are also connected to each other's laptops (to those of the people around you, your family and so on) both directly and via the internet. The link between your mental laptop and the world wide web of wisdom, so to speak, is quiet most of the time. Occasionally, however, messages appear on your screen unexpectedly, intruding on the programme you are already running. You can pay attention to the new messages or ignore them. Often, if you delete them, they seem to go away; but the *wisdom* mind is persistent, and will present the same messages to your everyday mind repeatedly, often in different guises; as a dream, for example, that stays with you on waking, or through some kind of meaningful coincidence.

Messages from the wisdom mind

The term Jung used for a meaningful coincidence was 'synchronicity'. It was an example of synchronicity that Kelly's mood changed coincidentally with the birth date of her lost pregnancy. It makes sense to pay attention to any unexpected communications we receive in this way, directly out of the unconscious. The most powerful such messages seem to be those transmitted in the form of pure, even raw, emotions. Kelly could not stifle or ignore her sorrow and tears, for example. When we pay attention to unexpected

---

[1] Carl Jung 1875 - 1961

emotions they can tell us a great deal about ourselves and our sticking points, as we shall explore and discover in later chapters.

It is possible to learn how to both maintain and improve the clarity of communication between our everyday minds and the wisdom mind. We can also improve our ability to interpret the messages we receive.

Although our first reactions, like Kelly's, are likely to feel negative, these communications can reliably be thought of as messages of love which bring healing. In serving to make broken relationships whole and heal emotional pain, making us complete, love improves our prospects of happiness. However, we need to be able to distinguish genuine messages from false ones. If we persistently run destructive programmes on our laptops; we can easily be led astray by others who may be sending appealing and persuasive but deceitful messages, invading our computers with a range of infective viruses.

The unfolding of wholeness

The remedy and guiding principle is love. "Love is the perfection of life", says the spiritual master Thomas Merton.[2] Perfection, in an important sense of the word, equates with wholeness and therefore with completion. This is a useful idea with which to unlock its true and full nature. A more achievable goal opens up when *to be perfect* is considered in the sense of *being complete*, rather than in the very different sense of *being without fault or flaw*.

The idea of completion suggests a process or several linked

---

2 In his book *Love and Living*, p35 . See 'Recommended Books and Websites'.

processes in operation, with definable transition and end points. In addition to the natural processes of healing, especially emotional healing, we will be concerned with those of growth towards personal and spiritual maturity throughout life.

The word 'whole' is linguistically linked with 'hale' (meaning healthy), health and healing, and has connections with 'holism' and with 'holiness'. It is good to remind ourselves from time to time that love has a sacred dimension. In serving to mend broken relationships, heal emotional pain and allow us to grow and mature as human beings, love improves our prospects of happiness.

These ideas form the starting point from which this book will unfold. It will be about the loving realm of the wisdom mind; opening ourselves to this universal mystery and becoming increasingly familiar with it. Learning how to penetrate and engage with this dimension of human experience enables our first responses of bewilderment, anxiety and rejection to convert naturally to those of reverence, joy, acceptance and peace, maximizing our chances of emotional health, happiness and maturity.

There is mystery, but there is logic to it: the holistic logic of healing and wholeness. For many, this is already a greater and more dominant logic than that of science, which it fully accepts and entirely incorporates. Grasp this holistic, 'non-dualist' logic pervading the universe and you will be on top of the game. It is the logic of love.

Reflections

Have you ever been surprised by a surge of emotion like Kelly's tears? What was its significance?

Are you aware of receiving helpful messages from your wisdom mind? If not, could it be that you have not yet found a way to tune in?

2. Spirituality and Health

There were no lectures on love when I went to medical school. There was no official mention then of compassion, wisdom, devotion or spirituality, but this is changing gradually. Because of its potential benefits, doctors are increasingly interested in the relevance of spirituality in the context of health care. There is increasingly reliable research evidence in most medical fields to back this up. [3]

Psychiatrists like me have been paying particular attention to this topic. In 1999, I was invited to help found the *Spirituality and Psychiatry* Special Interest Group (SIG) within the Royal College of Psychiatrists.[4] At the time of writing, we have over a thousand psychiatrists as members. The SIG is concerned to raise awareness of spirituality in mental healthcare for professionals, patients and their carers in three main ways: by encouraging the inclusion of spiritual concerns during psychiatric interviews; by enabling psychiatrists, in making a diagnosis, to be sensitive to the difference between spiritual crisis and mental illness, and where there may be overlap between the two; and by promoting knowledge of current research linking spirituality to improved physical and mental health.

---

[3] Extensively detailed, for example, in *The Handbook of Religion and Health.* See 'Recommended Books and Websites'.

[4] For further details of the SIG, see 'Recommended Books and Websites'.

What is spirituality?

We have discovered that the benefits of spirituality hold true whatever the identified religion of the patient. It seems important, then, to distinguish between spirituality and religion. Spirituality is not in itself the same as holding a particular religious belief, being religiously observant, or belonging to an established faith tradition. You can experience the spiritual dimension without any of these, and such experience tends robustly to be both inclusive and unifying. While there are many religions, spirituality is universal. As well as being universal, it is deeply personal, so it is experienced uniquely by each and every person. We say the spiritual dimension of human experience is the realm where the universal and the deeply personal meet.

Spirituality is like the roots and trunk of a tree, essential for anchoring and nourishing the branches and leaves, representing the different religions and their offshoots. It applies to everyone and seamlessly interconnects us all, including those who do not believe in God or any higher being. One of the important principles of spirituality is 'reciprocity', the basis for the golden rule, *to do as you would be done by*. According to this principle, harming another person is also somehow to do harm to oneself, and helping others is always somehow of benefit. Helping others, whether in the context of religious duty or not, can be thought of as a beneficial spiritual practice.

In the health care context, a person's spirituality can be thought of as his or her connection with the source of a deep-seated sense of meaning and purpose in life, together with both a sense of belonging and of harmony in the universe. Spirituality often involves seeking answers about the infinite, and is particularly important in times of stress, illness, loss, bereavement and death. Such concerns involve feelings, and are equally important for those with high or low levels of educational or social achievement. Nobody is exempt.

While relief of symptoms and, if possible, their eradication are important in health care, the primary aim from the spiritual perspective is towards the healing of the whole person. This often means that the person experiences adversity instead of avoiding it, in the process developing maturity through enduring hardship and transcending suffering. Life can be thought of as a journey involving not only the survival of pain and setbacks, but also growth through the ups and downs, the inevitable changes of circumstances and fortune which often, with hindsight, seem to have been necessary, even a blessing.

Spiritual health care

According to Mary Nathan, a nurse and researcher, psychiatric patients have identified the following five desirable factors in terms of spiritual health care:

- Having the opportunity to do something useful or pleasurable, such as creative art, structured work, and enjoying nature
- Being treated with respect and dignity, resulting in a feeling of belonging, of being valued and trusted
- Being able to express feelings to staff members while being listened to sympathetically
- Receiving encouragement to make sense of life's experiences,

including their illness

• Getting permission and encouragement to develop a relationship with God or the Absolute (however the person conceives whatever is sacred). This involves having a time, a place and privacy for prayer and worship, reflection and meditation, the opportunity to explore spiritual (and sometimes religious) matters, encouragement in deepening faith, feeling universally connected and perhaps also forgiven

The same patients identified the following benefits from receiving good quality care, including having appropriate attention paid to their spiritual needs:

• Improved self-control, self-esteem and confidence
• Faster, easier recovery, helped by the healthy grieving of loss, and the chance to attain one's full potential
• Improved relationships with self, others and with God, creation and/or nature
• A new sense of meaning to life, accompanied by the hope and peace of mind that help people accept and live with life's problems

As psychiatrists, we have been teaching ourselves to explore the religious and spiritual aspects of the lives of our patients. A helpful way to begin is to ask, "What sustains you through difficult times?' or simply, "What keeps you going?"

The answer to this enquiry usually reveals a person's main spiritual concerns and pursuits. There seem to be two important questions to consider: "What helpful *inner* personal resources can be encouraged?" and, "What *external* supports can the person rely on from the community, especially from his or her faith tradition or other spiritual support network?"

Relatively few people are used to talking openly about such matters, so we have found it best to approach the subject slowly and sensitively. Often, it will be more appropriate to invite the assistance of a chaplain or pastoral care adviser. Whoever tackles the issue, here are some questions that might be considered:

- Setting the Scene

What is your life is all about? Is there anything that gives you a particular sense of meaning or purpose?

- The Past

Emotional stress usually involves some kind of loss, or the threat of loss. Have you experienced any major losses or bereavements? How has it affected you and how have you coped?

- The Present

Do you feel that you belong and that you are valued? Do you feel safe and respected in a way that preserves your sense of dignity? Can you communicate freely? Does there seem to be a spiritual aspect to the current problems? Would it help to involve a minister of your faith, or someone from your faith community? What particularly needs to be appreciated about your religious background?

• The Future

What does the immediate future seem to hold? What about the longer term? Are you worried about death and dying, or about the possibility of an afterlife? Would it be helpful to discuss this more with someone? What are your main fears regarding the future? Do you feel the need for forgiveness about anything? What, if anything, gives you hope?

• Remedies

What would you find helpful? How might you find such help?

These are questions that people can also reflect on alone, and we have been generating leaflets containing them for distribution in psychiatric hospitals, day centres and other facilities. They could easily be modified for general health care settings, including hospitals and doctors' surgeries.

I have suggested to the medical students I teach that they ask one or two patients on medical and surgical wards about spiritual aspects of their lives, with particular reference to their health problems, using questions like these. The responses are highly consistent.

"When I asked him these questions, his eyes just lit up!" is a very common reaction reported by students, whose own eyes often light up as they speak about their encounters. They and their patients are clearly tapping into a wellspring of energy and vitality that seems certain to contribute helpfully to a person's general well-being; and many studies have shown that prevention of ill-health, as well as more rapid and more complete recovery from health problems, are associated with good levels of spiritual support and regular spiritual practice of some kind. In addition, people who report a satisfactory level of spiritual well-being are among those who are best able to endure illness-related pain and disability.

Spiritual skills, values and practices

The students say how different these conversations feel from their usual experiences of ward interviews focused mainly on symptoms, physical investigations and treatment. They say how often the patients express their genuine gratitude. Modern medicine and surgery are very specialized, tending to divide people into their constituent organs and parts. Interacting with the whole person by asking about spiritual issues can be rewarding for students and patients alike. We are keen, accordingly, to promote sensitively among students and health care workers what we refer to as spiritual skills, spiritual values and spiritual practices.

Spiritual skills include:

- Being able to rest, relax and create a still, peaceful state of mind
- Going deeper into that stillness, observing one's emerging thoughts and feelings with emotional stability in a way that carries an improved level of equanimity over into everyday life
- Using this capacity for deep reflection to connect with whatever you deem sacred and absolute – with God, with your soul, with the source of your core values – thus enabling additional

skills, including:

- Being honestly and sincerely self-reflective, taking responsibility for every thought, word and action
- Remaining focused in the present, staying alert, unhurried and attentive
- Developing compassion and an extensive capacity for direct empathic communication with others
- Being increasingly emotionally sensitive and resilient, thus having the courage to witness and endure distress while sustaining an attitude of hope
- Giving without feeling drained
- Being able to grieve and let go

The values identified through and promoted by this level of spiritual awareness include tolerance, patience, perseverance, honesty, kindness, compassion, creativity, wisdom, equanimity, hope and joy. All of these self-evidently support good health care practice.

Mutual benefit

An important principle of the spiritual approach to healthcare, already mentioned, is reciprocity, according to which givers and receivers of care *both* benefit. Provided exhaustion and 'burn-out' are avoided, care-givers naturally develop spiritual skills and values over time as a result of their devotion to those with whom they engage. Those cared for can often, in their turn, give help to others in distress.

Spiritual development can arise directly through working for the benefit of others, in whatever capacity. Work in health care, education and many other fields of human endeavour can be thought of as examples of spiritual practice. Such practices span a very wide range of human activity. Almost anything performed with a high degree of spiritual awareness and skill can be taken as a form of spiritual practice. Nevertheless, it can be helpful to make a list of the more obvious and common forms of spiritual practice; and this can be done by dividing the list into those practices which are 'mainly religious' in form and those which are 'mainly secular'. Doing this allows people who consider themselves 'not religious' to identify ways in which they are already engaged in spiritual practices as well as what they might do subsequently for the probable benefits.

List of spiritual practices
Mainly religious

- Belonging to a faith tradition
- Participating in faith community activities
- Attending and engaging in ritual and symbolic practices, and other forms of worship
- Going on pilgrimages and retreats
- Engaging in regular meditation and prayer
- Reading scripture
- Listening to, singing and/or playing sacred music, including songs, hymns, psalms and devotional chants

Mainly secular

- Acts of compassion (including work, especially teamwork)

- Deep reflection (contemplation)
- Yoga, Tai Chi and similar disciplined practices
- Engaging with and enjoying nature
- Contemplative reading of literature, poetry and philosophy
- Appreciation of the arts
- Engaging in creative activities, for example artistic pursuits, cookery and gardening
- Maintaining stable family relationships and friendships, especially those involving high levels of trust and intimacy
- Co-operative sporting, recreational or other group or team activities involving a special quality of fellowship

Research suggests that belonging to a faith community, holding religious or spiritual beliefs and engaging in associated practices are all helpful for both physical and mental health. This is why health care students and qualified clinicians are increasingly being taught about the value of patients' experiences of the spiritual dimension of life.

When, in turn, asked for advice, it is common to say that routine daily practice involving three elements can be helpful: regular quiet time for prayer, reflection or meditation; study of appropriate religious or spiritual material; and time spent with others of a similar spiritual outlook. More on this later in the book.

Reflections

Think about your own spirituality. Consider asking yourself the questions listed under the five headings on pages 22–23

What are the spiritual practices you engage in regularly?
Think about how you might develop your spiritual skills.

3. Losing Everything

Most readers will be aware of the Taoist yin-yang symbol. The yin principle is cool, dark, feminine and receptive. The yang principle, complementing it, is hot, bright, masculine and active. Each side contains at its heart the tiny seed of its opposite. The pictogram represents a philosophy of continuity, according to which opposites depend on each other, and the dynamic whole can only be appreciated when both are taken together.

This is an essential aspect of Tao, which means 'the Way' and refers to natural laws about the ways of the universe and the ways of humankind within it. The further you go towards or deep within something, the nearer you also reach the point of return, the reversal point of the pendulum swing. This development is inevitable. What seems dark makes way in time for the inextinguishable spark of purity within it flaring up once again into light. What seems bright eventually fades again similarly into darkness later, as the eternal cycle proceeds.

The true story of Viktor Frankl illustrates how the power of love works as an unquenchable glimmering force against the deepest darkness of merciless human destruction.

Born in March 1905, Frankl was a Viennese doctor, psychologist and director of a hospital neurology department when Austria was invaded by Hitler's National Socialists in 1938. Arrested by the Nazis in 1942, separated from his wife and family, Frankl was taken to a concentration camp. Eventually, after astonishing hardship, he survived. He was to live more than fifty fruitful years beyond the end of the war, dying in September 1997 at the age of 92.

Frankl continued to make psychological observations throughout his internment until liberation, developing ideas about survival under the heading of 'Logotherapy', a system of understanding and treatment that he had begun developing in 1926. Put simply, logotherapy has to do with finding meaning in life despite its changes in circumstances and fortune, in the process maintaining the will to live. Frankl's book *Man's Search for Meaning,* an account of his experiences, observations and conclusions, first published in 1946 and translated into several languages, has deservedly sold over nine million copies. [5] Although the story is a bleak one, it is particularly instructive in a number of ways. It tells us what can keep us alive and motivated when everything we value and rely upon is taken away.

At the time of his arrest, Frankl was a compassionate man and a healer. He had status and a career, a house, possessions, an income

---

[5] See 'Recommended Books and Websites'.

and probably savings, certainly ambitions, hopes and expectations regarding the future. He had also recently married a beautiful young wife. All these he was forced to give up. He was arrested by the Nazis for being Jewish, and so also had a faith and cultural tradition, although he does not emphasize this.

The reality of his predicament and his losses did not impinge upon Frankl fully at first. He was subject to protective denial. "Perhaps things are not as bad as they seem," we might have thought to ourselves, and said to each other in a similar situation. False hope, which Frankl calls 'the illusion of reprieve' persisted briefly, but the dark truth was quickly revealed.

The journey to the Auschwitz camp involved sharing a railway cattle truck with eighty others, fifteen hundred people on one train, the journey lasting several strength-sapping days and nights. On the final morning a huge internment camp became visible, with watchtowers prominent and surrounded by barbed wire. Long columns of dejected, rag-attired prisoners were being marched about the compound.

Frankl and his fellow travellers were told to leave their small amount of luggage on the train. This was everything that remained to them after leaving their homes at short notice, and would have contained the most precious of their objects, whether jewels or mementos. Frankl, unwilling to give it up, took a chance and hung on to his haversack containing the manuscript of his recent scientific book about logotherapy. Looking healthy and strong, he was sent to join a group of prisoners on one side of the station forecourt, while ninety per cent of the people from the train were ordered in the other direction. Soon this larger group went directly to the crematoria where everyone in it, women and children included, was killed and their bodies destroyed.

Frankl and the other survivors found out about this the same evening. Before the grim fact was made known, however, his group of men were made to run a good distance through the camp to the cleansing station, where they were ordered to remove their watches and jewellery. Frankl had to say goodbye to his manuscript then, in order to preserve his life. There was to be no mercy and, as he describes it, he was now forced for the first time by circumstances to face painful reality. The situation hopeless, he records the irrevocable moment when, in his mind: "I struck out my whole former life".[6]

The men were told to undress completely. They were then crowded together and shaved. All their body hair, including their eyebrows, was removed, and then they had a brief shower, as if to remove all trace of who they had once been. Numbers were tattooed into the skin of their arms, so they effectively lost even their names. Frankl was able to keep his spectacles and a pair of shoes, but everything else was obliterated. And yet, this was by no means the end for him. It was the start of three years of terror, hardship and the will to survive.

Who, reading this now, could imagine him or herself in such circumstances? All familiar activities and goals in life had been taken brutally away. Very little was left of personhood, of control, of dignity. We naturally hope that nothing similar will happen again, yet there are people today who encounter comparable circumstances,

---

[6] Man's Search for Meaning, p27.

and not necessarily under repressive regimes.

Imagine, for example, living peacefully in a place suddenly visited by natural disaster: a famine, an earthquake, a hurricane, a tsunami or a volcanic eruption. What would it be like?

Imagine also being told that you have cancer or some other potentially fatal disease. Your body is wasting. Your clothes no longer fit. You are debilitated and cannot go about your work or normal daily business. Imagine attending hospital for surgery, radiotherapy or chemotherapy. You are dressed in nightclothes and a hospital gown. A band is applied to your wrist with your name and hospital number on it. You might lose all your hair as a result of treatment, even your eyebrows. You experience pain, nausea and other unpleasant physical sensations. Like Frankl and others in Auschwitz, you too will have been stripped back to essentials. Important differences include that you are still in contact with your loved ones, and that the people around you want to help rather than destroy you. Nevertheless, it would be natural in the circumstances to feel frightened, helpless and very alone. Life-threatening illnesses and highly disruptive mental illnesses are with us and are common. Leukaemia and diabetes, like schizophrenia, affect young people.

If we are to help people suffering like this, it will be in part through giving them hope, and we can best do this by discovering and sharing with them that spark of vitality, that glimmering fire of love, present however dark a situation may seem. In their wholeness, our wisdom minds are connected to this divine source of energy, warmth and light. We each have the means, if not yet the skill, to make contact.

The first beneficial thing Frankl noticed in the concentration camp was humour. The naked and hairless men in the shower found themselves laughing at themselves and each other. Stripped completely bare, the human spirit shone through with remarkable strength and resilience. The laughter provided not only important relief, but also the beginnings of a bond between these unfortunate men. Helping each other continued to give meaning to an otherwise senseless existence during the next weeks and months.

As a folk saying has it, "A day without laughter and without tears is a day wasted". Laughter and crying, these are the two main ways we release emotional tension. These are forms of catharsis providing powerful, necessary and liberating connections between our true and false selves.

We laugh or cry when some previously unconsidered aspect of truth penetrates our awareness, bursting the bubble of denial. When we are ready to let go of the falsehood, we laugh. When we are still trying to hold onto it, but recognise that we cannot, we may grow angry, ashamed, frightened or confused; but in the end we will cry, as we are ultimately forced to let go. This is the process of healing. Releasing the energy bound up with our attachments, followed by reintegration and a sense of renewal: this is how we become whole again.

Frankl does not exactly say so, but I think the men were not only laughing at each other's bizarre new appearance, but also because of an unexpected sense of relief. When everything is taken from us, we are left with conscious awareness: with physical sensation – vision, hearing, touch, taste and smell – with emotional feeling, with powers of thinking, imagination and creativity; and with movement – or stillness – of the body. To have a shower then, to feel cleansing water stream over your naked flesh after days of exhausting travel in dirty, squalid conditions, would be restorative, healing mind and spirit through comforting and familiar bodily sensations. Such non-threatening experiences allow us to re-focus consciousness on the simple reality of the here and now. Our mind is full, if only for a brief moment, with nothing but physical sensations accompanied by a calming feeling of familiarity and comfort. In the case of Frankl and those with him, there was also relief that the showers were real and not issuing deadly gas.

The truth of such moments is like an incontrovertible fact, one that cannot be taken away by anybody. An ordinary shower can trigger a kind of remembrance of the deep-seated knowledge of that fact. It is like a soul-memory, and the ability to get in touch with that level of consciousness can form the basis of a powerful type of resilience. Furthermore, soul-memories are universal. They are shared. That seems to be why these men on their first grim day in Auschwitz found themselves laughing. They were forced, by the circumstances of having nothing else left, to make contact with their true selves; to get in touch, we might say, with their souls. Reports of their laughter may seem slightly macabre now, but then it was a healthy, spontaneous and necessary example of healing, the restoration of a sense of humanity and of motivation to struggle on against apparently impossible odds.

Frankl experienced many moments of despair whilst imprisoned in these death camps, but showed formidable resilience of body, mind and spirit. He describes several uplifting experiences that helped keep him going, as we shall see in the next chapter. In each case, to my mind, this was Frankl engaging with his wisdom mind to encounter his true self. But he also describes how important it was to have luck, fate, God or Providence on your side.

At this point it may be helpful to outline four levels of need that apply universally to all of us. Needs and desires are similar, but not the same. We can usually cope – if only by grieving – when our desires are not met, when we cannot have our own way; but needs are more important, essential in fact.

The levels of need referred to here overlap, of course. They may seem arbitrary, but they do allow us to think carefully through our values and priorities to decide and discover what gives meaning to our lives.

The first and most basic level of need concerns survival: food, clothing, safety and shelter. It is easy to think that all anyone really needs is the ability – in terms of funds, money, credit – to purchase these things; but we are wise to reflect on this in recognition that two stages are involved. Money does not automatically translate into getting our survival needs met. Being rich is no help in some circumstances – when you are lost in the wilderness, for example. Neither would it be any good were we to get our priorities wrong and spend our wealth unwisely, such as before stocking the larder. Conversely, as our ancestors knew, and modern bush craft experts demonstrate, survival with little money is possible when you know what you are doing.

The second level of need – once the basic elements of survival are securely and reliably catered for, once we have accommodation, sustenance and funds – concerns how we spend our time and who we spend it with. It has to do with occupation, recreation and relationships.

The third level of need gets us closer to thinking about what we want, rather than what is essential. This is the natural and entirely reasonable impulse for comfort, for a safety margin. It involves, say, storing up a little extra – in the food cupboard or the bank – as a protection against lean or difficult times ahead. This is prudent, but there is a risk with it: the danger of developing strong attachment to luxury and excess.

The fourth level of need begins with feelings of dissatisfaction even when the other needs are fully met. There is hunger for something missing, and the experience includes a powerful need to make sense of it all, to feel that there is a purpose to life, to all life, all creation, and to our particular individual life within it. This is the need for significance, for meaning and motivation, in what often seems like a meaningless world. I think of it as spiritual need.

Reflections

Can you imagine experiencing a situation in which you are cut off from family, friends and possessions?

How might you react? With resilience, humour and hope, or with hopelessness and despair?

4. Finding Hope

Ideally, each of our needs, at each level, must be fulfilled somehow to give life meaning and fuel a sense of purpose. "This is what I have to do today", we might tell ourselves in the morning. Working to meet our own needs, and those of others, gives life meaning on a day to day basis – more so than working simply to satisfy desires. We can think of this as spiritual meaning.

Choosing to live or to die

In the concentration camps, the overriding need every day was simply survival. Frankl, describing what was called 'barbed wire sickness', makes it clear that many survivors of the extensive initial Nazi culls gave their lives away afterwards. They ran into the electrically-charged fencing and so perished. They chose 'not to be" after reaching what I call 'the Hamlet point', rather than endure further "the slings and arrows of outrageous fortune". [7]

Frankl himself, on his first evening in the camp, made a firm and deliberate choice not to commit suicide. He decided 'to be'. This decision, for whoever takes it, requires courage. And when denial has been overruled by irrefutable reality, courage depends on a measure of faith, on the intuition that – although we are not able to see or experience it yet, and may never be able to – we do have a meaningful future. It helps to have faith that some kind of justice will eventually prevail. Courage and faith go together.

---

[7] Shakespeare 'Hamlet': Act 3, scene 1.

Hamlet's problem was that he did not see a worthwhile future for himself. Consequently, he lacked the necessary courage to make the fateful decision. Also, the manner in which he asks himself the key question suggests that it has to be answered only once. Sometimes this is enough. The commitment to being, to life, may be strong and absolute when it follows an authentic life-changing and life-enhancing experience. This, for example, is what seems to happen to Veronica, who we will meet in chapter 14. She tries to kill herself but fails. Soon afterwards, she comes to a new and more sympathetic understanding of herself. However difficult it had been so far, her life takes on new meaning and no longer feels like hers to throw away.

Sometimes the Hamlet question does not get resolved in one moment. It has to be faced repeatedly, even on a daily basis, possibly more often in hard times. People with addictions, such as to alcohol, when trying to change their destructive patterns of behaviour, have to rekindle their determination daily, even hourly when the craving is at its height. For them, it is essentially the same question: "To be; or not to be?" To stay sober or to drink to oblivion?

Frankl vividly describes how, in the concentration camps as conditions deteriorated, even in the final days before liberation at the end of the war, some people lost their will to survive. From a person's debilitated demeanour, it was even possible to predict accurately who was going to die next.

Survival needs

Having made the decision to live, come what may, and given the continuing fact of his survival, the main problems in the camps for Frankl concerned the perpetual and painful insistence of hunger and the need for food. Rations were meagre, so that even a small extra piece of bread could provide a momentary sense of comfort, almost of luxury.

After food came the necessity to conserve energy and rest when possible. Nature largely took care of this. A poor diet and hard physical labour in the work details left the men weak. They had, for example, no sexual energy or desire.

Physical hygiene was also important. Even though there were few opportunities to wash thoroughly, the men took turns grooming each other before sleeping at night, removing lice and other infestations from skin and re-growing hair. This reduced the irritation and helped them sleep better. Infections, such as typhus, also occurred in the camps and were often fatal. Survival chances improved with cleanliness and basic hygiene. Poor quality clothing and footwear often threatened health too. Clothes were little more than dirty rags, and shoes just increasingly tattered leather, poorly matched for size, often causing discomfort or actual pain, especially in the winter. A good pair of well-fitting shoes, or better still boots, was a genuine prize – but also a hazard, in case someone else, stronger and unprincipled, might want them.

It turns out that first level needs were closely connected in the concentration camp with level three needs relating to comfort (such little as might be available), security and protection. There was little protection from deprivation, violence and brutality, but it was essential to find favour with and avoid antagonising Nazi guards and the 'capos', prisoners given positions of trust and power over others. Frankl describes being treated in a life-saving way by one guard. The man spoke to him daily about his personal problems as they trudged the long distances to wherever the work details were sent. Frankl listened sympathetically and the guard was grateful.

On the other hand, inmates were sometimes beaten, or even shot on the spot, for a hostile glance or for no reason at all. Death was an ever-present reality. Frankl describes his strategy whenever dealing with someone in authority as staying silent until addressed directly. When answering questions, he always told the truth, but never said more than was necessary. This, he found, was the safest way of reducing the risk of provoking anyone.

Flattery or other ways of telling people what they wanted to hear; attempting to support and protect them in denial of the true situation; was risky. It could not be relied on to work. Guards suspecting someone of falsehood and of seeking special favours were quite likely to grow impatient and shoot them out of hand. It was a very tough school.

Support and attachment

The second level of need relates to occupation, recreation and friendship, but camp inmates had no need to find occupation. There was little respite from hard labour, building roads and railways from morning until night, day after day. Secondly, outright friendship between prisoners was problematic. A kind of grim camaraderie and mutual support became important as one of the pinions of survival, but if you made a friend, he might be moved to a different hut or work gang. He might die of sickness or be killed; so people protected themselves from getting too close, from the risk of losing such a fragile source of affection. Although extremely overcrowded, the barracks were essentially lonely places. Frankl tells us that he liked it best when he could be alone in a quiet secluded place, sheltered near one of the huts, even for just a few minutes' respite and reverie. He yearned to be alone with his thoughts and dreams. It was necessary, he said, part of the process of keeping hope somehow alive.

But this was not the whole story. Without seeming to emphasize the point, as if taking it for granted, Frankl frequently intimates that helping another to survive is as important and natural as saving oneself. "All efforts and all emotions," he writes, "are centred on one task: preserving one's own life and that of the other fellow". [8]

This is not the same as friendship. Such a degree of loyalty speaks of identification. When we 'identify' with someone, some group or some thing, such as an idea or ideology, this is a close, intimate, even seamless level of attachment. It is very powerful and, because often automatic and unconscious, we tend to take such identifications for granted. It may seldom occur to us to take note of and reflect upon the people, objects and ideas with which we are identified; but these are attachments which define us, which both enthral and control us, and we do well to take the time and trouble to ponder them occasionally.

Occupation, then, in the form of hard labour, was arduous and entirely controlled by camp officials. Despite strong identifications and loyalties, personal friendships were difficult to establish and maintain. And whereas recreation was also challenging, it was not ruled out entirely.

Time, strength and the opportunity for games, sports or artistic

---

[8] Man's Search for Meaning, p40.

activities were generally lacking, but entertainment of a sort was available. Inmates often shared and enjoyed songs, poems and jokes, in a way that helped Frankl and the others forget their circumstances, their hunger and fatigue, their pains and sicknesses, their isolation and loneliness, their many losses and uncertainty about the future. Re-creation is about renewal of the spirit as well as resting the body and revitalising the mind. In this sense, all three levels of need covered so far are subsumed into the fourth, spiritual level: the need for significance, meaning and motivation.

Spiritual meaning: Frankl's epiphany

Frankl was impressed by the strong degree of interest in religion among camp prisoners, many of whom demonstrated deep, vigorous and moving levels of belief and expression. Prayers and short services were often improvised. In the extreme circumstances of concentration camp life, when possessions are taken away and life is stripped to the barest of essentials, ultimate truths are within easier reach than in more normal conditions. Frankl described carefully the deepening and intensification of his own inner, spiritual life as he searched for and discovered hope.

In his case, he took strength especially from memories of his wife and their love for each other. Frankl had no news of his wife while he was in the camp, and did not know if she was alive or dead. Nevertheless, holding her in his imagination frequently, often for long periods, he found solace and, eventually, something more: a kind of enlightenment. The thought transfixed him one day that, for each of us, love is the ultimate and highest goal to which we can aspire. The reciprocal love between himself and his wife seems to have expanded into a universal love for humanity and creation. This is what he says:

> "I grasped the meaning of the greatest secret that human poetry and human thought and belief have to impart. *The salvation of man is through love and in love.* I understood how a man who has nothing left in the world still may know bliss." [9]

This seems to be his still-point, a timeless moment during which Frankl encountered his true self, his soul. We can call it an 'epiphany'. Part of the wisdom awakened within him then was the sure knowledge that love is transcendent. It goes beyond the physical person. It does not depend on their presence, or on whether they are still living or not. Love for a person depends on the spiritual reality of each, on what extends into this extra dimension from our physical selves. This is not a point that can properly be understood by thought processes alone. It is, as it was for Frankl, a matter of the most profound, transformational personal experience. The hidden life force, the ember of love was rekindled by these moments of contemplation.

Frankl also describes the power of beauty. He writes of the palpable wonder and joy on the faces of his fellow inmates on beholding through their prison bars, for example, the glory of mountain peaks glowing in a sunset. Sometimes his own experiences were even more mystical. One day, for example, when working under guard in a grey dawn landscape, feeling somewhat

---

[9] Frankl's italics. Man's Search for Meaning, p49.

numb, his mind again questioning and resisting the apparent senselessness of his existence, he suddenly as it were 'heard', filling his mind and his entire soul, a triumphant affirmative: the word 'Yes'. At the exact moment, a light was lit in a farmhouse in the distance, as if to confirm the fact of a sacred light "shining in the darkness"[10]. This is the light that cannot be overcome, a powerful message of hope.

This description goes beyond thought, involving the whole psychological being of the person – senses, thoughts and emotions – and it can happen to anyone. There is no impulse to act, because the entire experience is one of *being acted upon* by some great and loving power. You feel yourself to be in a state of acceptance, of grace and gratitude, of insight and understanding, of peace. In an instant, your life becomes full, complete, and bursting with meaning, with the significance of knowing yourself part of and at one with a perfect, timeless, infinite and eternal whole, an indescribably sacred unity, an infallible source of hope. The Hamlet question immediately becomes redundant. Life is no longer about being or non-being. The two are subsumed into one: being *and* non-being. This works because having once been, you cannot be obliterated. You leave an imprint, an ineradicably secure trace in the realm of the human spirit.

Frankl goes on to describe vividly how often he and others were faced with real questions like Hamlet's, and daunting, life-or-death decisions. These included decisions about whether to try and escape, for example, or whether to accept transfer to a rest camp,

---

[10] A reference to the Bible: St John Ch 1: Vs 5.

where conditions were said to be better, but may in fact have been much worse. Indeed, sometimes volunteers for the so-called 'rest camp', a place intended to allow men to recover their strength before returning to hard labour, were taken away and unceremoniously murdered.

With his hope, faith and courage rekindled, Frankl tells us that he always preferred not to try and calculate the odds, but to let fate take its course at such times. Either intuitively or through the hand of Providence, he seemed to be in the right place each time to survive. This was almost miraculously true, particularly towards the end of the war when life became even more hazardous. Camp officials were under great pressure either to exterminate people faster or to seek safety for themselves. The latter often meant neglecting conditions regarding food and sanitation in the camps, with predictable consequences.

Viktor Frankl survived. Sadly, though, his wife, parents and brother were all holocaust victims. Frankl soon became director of the Vienna Neurological Policlinic, a post he held for twenty-five years after the end of the war. It is said to have taken him only nine days to dictate the account that became his enormously bestselling book. Love helped him survive the camps, and happily revisited him after the liberation too. He met a young hospital worker and fell in love with her. She became his second wife in 1947.

The fear of being nobody

The dark of Nazi hatred and unspeakable intolerance led to the ruthless extermination of Jews, homosexuals, the mentally ill, and those thought of as either 'feeble-minded' or otherwise physically handicapped; all of whom were people capable of loving and of being loved. But this institutionalized enmity was ultimately penetrated by the unquenchable and inexhaustible fire of love. Frankl's case is only one example. Very many acts and sacrifices were made in the name of love, of faith and reverence for justice, to overturn the Nazi menace and bring freedom from extreme partisan oppression. But where had this menace come from?

The fanatical prejudice exemplified by Hitler and his Nazi followers was, from a psychological perspective, a negative aspect of the need we all have for meaning and significance. This intense fear of meaninglessness is a common factor underlying totalitarian doctrine wherever it holds sway. We will see later how it is natural during childhood, at an early stage of individual psychological and spiritual development, to think of the external world as a continuation or extension of ourselves. This gives us a protective, but false, sense of omnipotence. We have become egocentric and feel in control, capable of manipulating people and situations to our wilful purposes; and dictators are often somehow stuck at this stage. They depend too on many people being fixed also at a similarly immature stage during which, not yet confident enough and ready to take responsibility for ourselves, we seek out a strong, protective and guiding force or person to follow – and to follow uncritically.

The effect of this combination; a strong, dictatorial and rigidly partisan leader with a mass of uncritical, intensely (and misguidedly) loyal followers; is conflict and destruction. Hitler and the Nazis give us an example of people showing what, in maturity, we can identify clearly as an extraordinary level of presumption, judging themselves superior to all and identifying themselves as the master race. Interviewees from that period of German history have said, for example, "We were presented with a perfect world. We were in the grip of unbridled pride. We were somebody".[11] This type of sentiment reveals denial on a mass and therefore dangerous scale, reflecting a profound fear and abhorrence of insignificance, of being nobody.

It is, however, an extreme insult to the true self to find meaning and purpose from the heartless extinction of even one person deemed to be second-rate. This seems obvious. It is too simple, and too transparently false a solution, to gain our own significance by perceiving others, those who are somehow different, as inferior. Nevertheless, as we shall see in more detail as we explore personal development in later chapters, we all go through the various stages of moral and spiritual growth, and are subject to such thoughts and impulses ourselves, until we mature and see through them. That is why such thinking, driven by fear and anger rather than by inner peace, acceptance and love, is surprisingly common. It surfaces especially at times of perceived threat, at both the personal and communal levels. It may not lead to murder in every case, but it can still put us in spiritual danger, because it leads inevitably to partisanship and so to intolerance, bullying, cruelty and victimisation in all their forms. If we learn about it, we will have better chances of ending and preventing recurrences of unacceptable authoritarian and partisan persecution, wherever it may be found.

---

[11] Adapted from a BBC television documentary, 'Nazis: A Warning from History', broadcast on 4th June 2005.

Reflections

What sustains you in adversity?

What helps you most when life gets tough?

5. Mysteries of the Universe

The wisdom mind is a mystery. Western philosophy has seldom grappled effectively with a holistic concept of reality. Wittgenstein, the celebrated twentieth century philosopher[12], may have come closest when he wrote in his book *Tractatus Logico-Philosophicus*, "Whereof one cannot speak, thereon one must be silent".

He had reached what he considered the limits of human understanding, while recognizing something more, something inexpressible, to be true. The phrase 'Whereof one cannot speak' denotes mystery. There are mysteries beyond logic and reason that affect everyone in a deep and universal way. Our response to them may not be verbal, but it can be emotional. My response to Wittgenstein is: Whereof we cannot speak, thereat we may well be amazed.

Too mysterious for words

Who has not discovered the beauty, wonder and inspiration to be found in the unspoken mysteries of creation; a sunset, for example, a thunderstorm or the flight of birds? We may react with awe and wonder, fear and trembling, joy and gratitude; with the entire spectrum of human emotional life. If we are alive, we will respond to whatever is new to us and apparently unexplained. Because they are central to life and living and to death and dying, we need to communicate about these feelings, sharing what knowledge and wisdom we can. If we want to feel in control, and do not want our

---

[12] Ludwig Wittgenstein 1889 - 1951

everyday minds disrupted frequently by the effects of powerful emotions, we need intelligently to understand as much as we can. That is the rationale for science.

The mission of science is to demystify the things and events we experience with our everyday minds. It is systematic in its approach to investigating the objects of its enquiry. It necessarily divides seamless existence into parts and particles, the continuum of reality into more or less discrete episodes and moments. Science does not require an idea of indivisible wholeness. It seeks beginnings and endings, measurable boundaries, categories of phenomena. The absolute, the infinite and the eternal are beyond the capacity of its methods to investigate, so some of those engaged in scientific activities are tempted to ignore, even deny the relevance of this mysterious dimension, referred to here as the 'spiritual' dimension. Although not directly accessible to either science or reason, this dimension can be contacted through direct perception, when messages from the wisdom mind break through into everyday consciousness; and, for example, through meditative intuition.

Five dimensions of human experience

How can we reconcile science with spirituality? I do not see much of a problem. It is a matter of 'both/and' thinking, rather than 'either/or'. We can approach the question systematically by describing five interconnected dimensions of human experience: physical, biological, psychological, socio-cultural and spiritual. Science works best with the first two: the plane of material existence, explained by physics and chemistry, and that of living organisms, explained by biology. Even here, apparently impenetrable mysteries continue to operate, as we shall see.

Dimensions of Human Experience
Physical

Biological

Psychological (intra-personal)

Socio-cultural (inter-personal)

Spiritual

These are not separate categories. The five seamlessly inter-related dimensions in the list are arranged in a hierarchy. Physical objects are formed from the interplay of energy, sub-atomic particles, atoms and molecules, according to the sciences of physics and chemistry. The biological sciences, dealing with living creatures, reveal a more complex level of organisation.

Emerging from the biology of our inseparable brains and bodies, the activities of our minds – including consciousness itself – are more complex still. This makes them difficult to study in individuals with the aim of achieving reproducible results. That explains why the science of psychology is one of populations. Its findings are usually expressed as probabilities, rather than of reproducible certainties. This is also true at the next level of organisation, the socio-cultural dimension.

So far, to some extent, each level can be explained according to the phenomena of the previous level. There is, though, a qualitative difference in each case that cannot be explained. How do chemicals in complex combinations give rise to life? How does the organ of the brain give rise to conscious awareness? Some people argue that science has explained these satisfactorily, however there remains a degree of mystery.

A teaching story about wisdom

Here is another story, one that was first recorded a long time ago. Although there is no reason why it should not feature a mother and daughter, it happens to be about a loving father teaching wisdom to his eager, intelligent and respectful son.

One day the father asked his son to fetch a fruit from a large tree, a banyan, instructing him then to break open the fruit and say what was inside it. 'Very small seeds, Sir,' replied the son, at which his father asked him to break open one of the seeds. 'What do you see inside it?' he asked. 'Nothing at all,' was the son's slightly puzzled reply.

'And yet, although you cannot see it,' his father continued, 'within that seed lies the source of a magnificent and productive fruit tree. The whole universe is something like that. A subtle, invisible yet powerful and creative essence, a spirit of sacredness, pervades it all.'

The son wanted to know more, so his father showed him a container of water and beside it a pile of salt. 'Put the salt in the water tonight, and come and see me again tomorrow morning,' he said.

The next day the father asked his young son to bring him the salt, but of course the boy could not find it in the water. He was told by his father to taste the water, and to sample it from each side of the container, whereupon he declared that wherever he tasted from, the taste was salty. 'But I cannot see the salt, Father,' he said. 'I can only see the water.'

'In the same way, my darling Son,' replied his father, 'You cannot see the Spirit, but I assure you truthfully, it is here. This subtle and invisible essence is the spirit of the whole. . . of the whole universe. That is Reality. That is Truth. . . And you are part of it too.'

This is one of the first stories ever to have been written down. It was recorded in Sanskrit, the ancient language of Hindu people in India. The story is from the one hundred or so 'Upanishads'[13], most of which were composed between 800 and 400 years BCE. The word 'Upanishad' has a meaning connected with the idea of sitting at the feet of a revered teacher, so this wisdom story is from a collection of the earliest sermons or wisdom talks that we have.

Today, of course, a father would have to ask his son to look into the flesh of the banyan seed with a microscope to see the individual plant cells of which it is constituted. He would then have to show his son higher power magnification photographs and illustrations to demonstrate nuclei within the cells and the chromosomes they contain. These, he would explain, are made up of molecules of DNA, the coding for the genetic material which gets passed on from one generation to the next, determining the characteristics of the offspring. He would explain that all living creatures, plants and animals have self-replicating nucleic acids in their cells, and that a mechanism exists for mixing chromosomes from different types of organism, male and female, to ensure variety.

---

[13] See 'Recommended Books and Websites'

The uncertainty principle

But even this exploratory investigation into the true and ultimate nature of physical and living entities does not end here. The father is also obliged to show his son that long-chain molecules like DNA are made up of large numbers of individual atoms of different types, and that these contain smaller entities still, the protons, neutrons and electrons.

'And what are these made of?' The son might ask. 'Well, to tell you truthfully', the father might reply, 'It is an unavoidable mystery. Smaller particles have been discovered, but they are too small to be seen by even the most powerful microscope. Single atoms are about one ten-thousand-millionth of a centimetre in diameter. They cannot be visualised, and are only known by their effects in highly specialised experimental conditions. It is like when you look with the naked eye into the flesh of the seed. You cannot pin down satisfactorily the composition of these exotic smaller particles. Some of them have been given names like 'quarks' and 'gluons', but they are essentially unstable on their own. We cannot explain fully in terms of fundamental physical material the miracles of existence and the miracle of life.'

'We have theories, of course,' the father may continue. 'Currently, much in favour are quantum foam theory, superstring theory and M theory (where M stands for membrane). But when we look closely at sub-atomic particles, things seem to get a bit strange. It is as if by looking we are affecting what it is we are looking at, so it is no longer possible to be sure how to interpret our observations. This is known as the 'Uncertainty Principle'. The universe protects its secrets from us in this way.'

The matter making up atoms and molecules contains and is also effectively composed of enormous amounts of energy. Einstein revealed many years ago that, under certain conditions, according to his well-known equation, $e=mc^2$, matter and energy are interchangeable. It has, nevertheless, been calculated that only five per cent of the universe is made up of atomic material. The remaining mass and energy has not yet been detected. It is a cosmic mystery; but so-called 'dark matter' is said to comprise seventy-five percent of the universe and 'dark energy' about twenty per cent.

'I do not expect you, Son, to comprehend these figures fully or what is behind them. But I want to assure you,' the father might continue, 'that none of this invalidates what I told you earlier about a pervasive and subtle essence or Spirit inhabiting the universe.'

The glory in the banyan seed

'This essence is everywhere at once. It is in the tiniest sub-atomic particle and throughout the vastness of space. It moves instantaneously, faster than the speed of light. Physicists have observed that particles far apart can affect each other simultaneously throughout the universe. This has yet to be explained satisfactorily, but you may take comfort in the mystery. It is not only in matter and energy, both, but is also behind and beyond matter and energy. It is that from which they are formed.

Outside time, it has no beginning and no end. Although people have called it by many names, it has no true and proper name – for to give it a name would be to reduce it once more to the realm of things, and therefore of thinking. This would be to falsify it; to render it incomplete. Our minds are part of the whole, but when we try reducing that whole to a single thought or a single word by giving it a name, we take the great risk of belittling it, and of confusing ourselves.'

'In itself, dear Child, this essence has no substance. It is void. It is no-thing. But it is not nothing. It is *every* thing. It is everything. And you can experience it. You can, even if only fleetingly, experience becoming one with it, because you and I and all the people are already at one with it. Our task is to realise that; to make it real, to make it our reality. This is the sacred reality we own and are owned by.'

The father continues, 'This breath, this spirit inhabits us. Moment by moment, it forms us. At the deepest level, it is us – and we are it. There is no need to be afraid of what I am telling you, beloved Son. Nothing has changed since I started speaking, since you came to me with the banyan seed last evening, or since you placed salt in the container of water. What I am speaking of is our glory, not only the glory of humankind but also of all creation. If you do not know it is there, it will be hard for you to seek it out, to bring it forth in your life and in the lives of others. That is why I am telling you this.'

'You have to taste the water to discover the salt. When you have similarly experienced the spirit, you become free to develop a secure faith in human spirituality and the divine essence. From such faith comes courage, the courage to seek out this spirit each moment and live by its truth until the end of your days. That, dearest Child, is my desire for you, my sacred wish for your happiness and contentment. Then you will have inner peace, joy and contentment. Your life will be a blessing for others. Take this banyan seed as a token and perpetual reminder.'

The spiritual dimension seems to both underpin and surpass the other main dimensions: physical, biological, psychological and socio-cultural. Spirituality is that which seamlessly connects every part with the whole. Where humans are concerned, it involves intimate links between what is both deeply personal and universal. This is why it is essential to consider it with respect to human psychology.

Spirituality has to do with a silent and invisible energizing and connecting principle. It defeats exploration and examination using the methodologies of science, and so seems to have been largely forgotten by serious thinkers. Only now is it beginning to regain its prominence as a topic of enquiry and general discussion[14]. The spiritual realm is a realm of silence, but should we be silent about it? Probably not.

Reflections

Is everything about the physics, chemistry and biology of human life understood?

Does anyone know how the brain gives rise to conscious awareness? Do you think we will ever get to the bottom of these mysteries?

---

[14] Described, for example, in *The Spirituality Revolution* by David Tacey. (See 'Recommended Books and Websites')

6. The Yin and Yang of Emotions

Many people think of 'things' in terms of objects, as if all things were of solid matter, both visible and touchable. The word 'thing', however, may be related to the word 'thinking'. So, arguably, things are more like 'thinks'. This means that every thing we can do or know about owes an important aspect of its existence to human consciousness. By the same token, human consciousness owes an important aspect of its existence to every thing that exists, to everything. The yin/yang of consciousness holds and is held by the corresponding yin/yang of creation.

We can see this by looking at a simple overview of the timeline of the universe, starting from the Big Bang and eventually arriving at human life. First, we will look more closely at the central idea that the reality we inhabit is a seamless totality to which we are each indivisibly linked by our breath, by simply being alive.

This holistic idea, linking breathing with the sacred totality of existence, has been widespread in many cultures throughout world history. The Latin word for 'breath' is *spiritus* from which the word 'spirit' is derived. There are many languages in which breathing and spirit are related by a single word. In Chinese the word is *chi* (as in *tai chi*), in Hebrew *ruach*, in Aramaic *ruha* and in Sanskrit *prana*. These words are also sometimes used equally to mean 'air', 'wind' and 'life force'. It does not seem to matter what we call it, this vital essence, as long as we accept that something powerful and mysterious is at work in our lives. It is something unknowable in the conventional sense, but accessible directly through the finely tuned faculties of wisdom mind.

There are few cultures with no tradition or story about this. We tend to be curious about and respond to narrative accounts in adulthood, but children especially love such stories and respond well to them, intuitively grasping their messages of collected and collective wisdom. A child may be able to read, but the ideal occurs when stories are told sympathetically and with love by a parent or some other adult whom they trust. We have already seen this in the context of instruction given by the father to his young son in the ancient Hindu Upanishads. How wonderfully he engaged his son in the process of discovery.

For this father, the narrative clearly involved the most important wisdom he could impart. The same guiding principle about a universal spirit has similarly been respected and passed on from generation to generation until more recent secular times. The same holistic truth is still to be found pervading the many related but distinct traditions from the East – Taoism, Jainism, Buddhism (especially Zen Buddhism) and the contemporary Advaita (non-duality) interpretation of Hinduism. It is there too in the mystical versions of Judaism, Christianity and Islam. The time seems ripe now for its rediscovery.

Rediscovering wholeness

If we put every separate thing together with every other thing, we get the totality. We get unity. We get indivisibility. We get wholeness.

This is Perfect.

That is Perfect.

Perfect comes from Perfect.

Take Perfect from Perfect

And the remainder is Perfect.

This wisdom from the Upanishads encapsulates the holistic principle. It cannot be damaged or smashed. Imagine sticking your hand into a large three-dimensional yin-yang symbol. Make a fist and withdraw a portion. Open your fist and look. There you will find a perfect yin-yang symbol, a small replica of the original. Look back at that original and you will see it once again whole.

This is an important image or thought-experiment because ordinarily, by the process of thinking, we cannot help but divide the whole (in our minds) back into parts, into apparently separate things. It is immensely useful to be able to do this, but we are wise to remain mindful of the ultimately indivisible whole from which every thing, and every thought, is derived.

When we lose touch with a sense of the whole, we risk making mistakes. If you usually think of things as solid, visible and touchable; of something material, rather than as part of something boundless and eternal; confusion may follow. This is not a cause for great concern, because it is natural. Confusion has an emotional component, as we shall see, and remains part of the bigger picture, part of the whole.

Although uncomfortable, it is normal to feel confused sometimes, because the emotion of bewilderment arises naturally whenever things seem to go awry, whenever we feel in some way under threat. Later, we shall look more closely at what specifically is under threat when our thoughts, our ideas and our understanding are challenged.

People naturally become bewildered whenever things seem to go wrong or awry. Notice the word 'seem'. Sometimes things *seem* to go wrong when in the bigger picture all remains satisfactory. Things are fine, but we are not yet able to see and appreciate that point. Our emotional reactions get in the way; so this type of situation provides us with an opportunity to adjust our perception and thinking, to learn something, to improve our understanding of things and so grow, to mature a little in wisdom.

That is why it can be good to feel bewildered occasionally. Whatever stage of life we have reached, this means that we are still maturing, developing, growing. It can be an exciting experience, the type that for many people gives life meaning. This is also why it can be useful, even necessary, to make mistakes. They give us really good opportunities to learn.

It is relatively easy to think of something like a banyan, or a single grass seed, and multiply it in our mind's eye. From one we can imagine many, a handful, a bucketful, a warehouseful, even more. We can imagine spreading the many seeds over a prepared earthen surface, and we can imagine a huge orchard or vast lawn resulting from this action. But the universe is filled with more than banyans and turf.

Emotional reactions and our whole being

As we conceive it, the universe contains many things. To make the whole more manageable, we think of these things (these 'thinks') as belonging to different categories, a category being a group of things to which we mentally ascribe some attribute in common. Not only are there many, many things in the known universe, but we can also delineate very many categories of thing. To suggest that the many things of many categories in the known universe are somehow seamlessly interwoven into one complete unity, into some kind of super-huge whole, each part of which affects and is affected by each other part, is a challenging idea; but this is the spiritual vision, the view of non-duality.

The idea challenges us because we are tempted to think about this whole as if it were just another thing. It is not. The totality is different, because we cannot appreciate it in the same way as we do parts or particles. For one thing, we cannot think of it similarly because it has no easily discernible boundaries, either in space or time.

We cannot consider the totality of existence in the same way that we think about grass or banyan seed. Whenever we think we can and attempt to, we risk making harmful mistakes. Each person, however, has opportunities to find other, more complete and satisfying ways to engage with this whole of which we are each an indivisible and individual part. Instead of thoughts and thinking, the qualitatively different method required will necessarily involve our whole being. It will be an experience or set of experiences that involve each person's entire personality, and especially the emotions. We can try to ignore this totality, but it continues to influence us. To reject it is to reject our true selves and live an incomplete life. When someone begins to embrace the totality, however, faith and courage come into play together with love, healing and happiness.

We mostly like doing what we are good at and avoiding what we are less good at, so it is natural to resist trying to master this seemingly insuperable conundrum: what is the nature of the whole of existence? If you have learned to trust only rational, logical thinking, rather than what we might call poetic or intuitive thinking, it would be normal at this stage to feel bewildered, even a little frustrated, impatient and angry; but note that these are emotional reactions, and it is often emotion that obstructs the clarity of our thoughts. I am going to try and demonstrate the way through this problem.

If we try to think about the great, timeless, seamless, indivisible, indestructible, infinite hugeness that is the whole universe, we cannot fully encompass it with our minds because there is no end to it. We are easily bewildered by the attempt, and may quickly give up on it; but perseverance is recommended. Relatively few people from a modern, westernised, essentially secular culture have the necessary skills to perceive the whole deal. They are not prioritized, so people remain relatively unhappy, chasing the false gods of power, wealth and fame; but these skills can be acquired, and some can be taught to children. It takes training to develop an ability or talent we all have, at least in rudimentary form, and this will involve both personal discipline and spiritual maturity. Immaturity in these matters is not to be criticised, though. This simply means that a person is still ripening, still travelling towards perfection. No one breathing has yet reached the completion of his or her journey through life.

Let me introduce a useful way of considering emotions. This is a scheme that permits an explanation of emotional healing. It reveals the outcome of such healing, not in terms of restoration of a previous equilibrium, but in terms of personal growth and the gradual development of spiritual maturity. This makes it a scheme full of hope.

Doing emotional algebra

The natural relationship between clarity and bewilderment demonstrates a pattern that is repeated with other pairs of emotions. It goes like this: a clear mind is not bewildered, and a bewildered mind is not clear. A similar relationship holds too, for example, between calm and anxiety. The more one affects a person at any given moment, the less does the other. This is automatic. The relationship between any pair of such complementary emotional experiences can be thought of as algebraic. They balance each other. Their sum is unity. If emotions could be measured precisely, the amount of calm (C) and the amount of anxiety (A) would follow the formula C plus A equals unity ($C + A = 1$). It is not necessary to follow the mathematics of the equation, only the principle.

According to the principle, as with clarity and bewilderment, calm and anxiety are not two separate entities but two aspects – like yin and yang – of the same whole. We call this a 'dyad'. This point is important because, although anxiety and bewilderment are unavoidable, calm and clarity are obviously preferable. The former are relatively painful; the latter relatively pain-free or pleasurable. Recognising the pattern, and understanding how these emotions operate in this interdependent way, gives us an advantage. It improves our chances of influencing our emotions in the direction we would like to experience them: away from pain and towards pleasure.

Emotional clarity, the absence of bewilderment, enables truly clear thinking. This is the pure kind of mental activity that leads directly to discernment and wisdom. It is more than just the ability to calculate. This kind of clarity allows our intuitive and creative faculties to operate freely.

What is emotional health? This is a complex question, but it seems to me to involve being able to experience both painful and pleasurable aspects of a wide spectrum of emotions while retaining a stable equilibrium, with the balance on the pain-free side. The healthier you are the greater intensities of emotion you can experience and tolerate, including extremes of both joy and distress. In this way, you are likely on a daily basis to feel more alive. You will be rich in experience and relatively untroubled by fear. This, too, is an aspect of spiritual maturity. Any person retaining a calm and alert equanimity in the face of danger and loss will also be of great value to others.

Where there is limited equanimity, and bewilderment prevails to an extent we begin to find irksome, some form of emotional healing is required before we can start thinking clearly again. We will be looking at emotional healing according to this scheme more closely later, and in doing so we will need to examine other emotions in order to understand how they interact. Bewilderment, for example, is close to and linked particularly with both doubt and anxiety, so these emotions can also affect the clarity of our thinking.

Working toward emotional health

Here is the spectrum of emotions that we are going to work with:

Painful	Pain-free
Wanting (desire/dislike)	Contentment
Anxiety	Calm
Bewilderment	Clarity
Doubt	Certainty
Anger	Acceptance (non-anger)
Shame	Worthiness
Guilt	Innocence (purity)
Sadness	Joy

Without a guide or a reliable system, it is easy to get confused on the subject of emotions. There are drawbacks to this scheme, but I recommend setting them aside for now in the interests of clarity.

For those who prefer to be scientific in their approach to understanding natural phenomena, there are one or two points to be made. One is that we cannot directly or accurately measure emotions like bewilderment or anxiety. We can measure biological concomitants – such as skin conductance and heart rate – but emotions are primarily subjective experiences. This subjective part cannot be accessed directly, except in ourselves. Part of the problem here is that thinking about emotional experiences while having them interrupts and alters them. A kind of uncertainty principle is involved. To try and recall emotional experiences later also introduces the possibility of inaccuracy. This may be a helpful exercise in the course of research; during which for example large numbers of people are given questionnaires to establish a range of reactions and average responses to given situations; but only approximate rather than precise values can be assigned.

Emotional states can change rapidly, moment by moment, both in nature and in intensity. There is no 'real time' way of recording and measuring these changes, so there cannot be a 'pure' science of emotion. Subjectivity and the interpretation of observations necessarily apply. This need not be an insuperable problem, however, for it prompts a change of direction in our search.

Science has tended to look 'out there', seeking objectivity and reproducible facts. The emotions, and other psychological phenomena, have usually been studied on groups of people to obtain the best approximation of truth through multiple observations. Another, more intimate and meaningful way would be for people to develop the capacity to explore 'in here', to find the truth about ourselves using less scientific, more 'contemplative' methods. This type of observation is both immediate and incontrovertible, at least for the person concerned. It is quite possible to train people to investigate their own minds, and to do so in a reasonably reliable way. As with other human activities, some will have a more natural aptitude and a greater inclination to improve their skills in this regard than others. Allowing such people to come together and communicate their experiences might well yield valid and valuable results.

This seems to be an experiment that humanity has already started. It began a long time ago, perhaps with the writers of the Upanishads and their predecessors. It has continued with their successors in many different cultures to the present day, and what we get is closer to wisdom than reproducible scientific knowledge.

Reflections

Try to think about the great, timeless, seamless, indivisible, indestructible, infinite hugeness that is the entire universe. What is its essence?

Think of all the opposites within it interacting like yin and yang, ultimately cancelling each other out.

7. Stories about our Origins

Human existence is amazing! Here I sit breathing, pausing at the word processor, immobile for a few seconds, looking through the nearby window at sunlight-dappled trees swaying in a gentle breeze, vivid with colour. I hear only silence. Now there is the soft drone of a light plane passing high above. My senses are alert, my mood tranquil, my everyday thoughts suspended. In this moment, I simply exist. Meanwhile, some part of my awareness is also marvelling at the fact. My heart is joyful.

Turning back to writing this chapter, I want to say something about the stories we tell about our origins, about how we come to be who, what and where we are. These stories fulfil profound needs for meaning and a sense of belonging. These are spiritual needs.

A satisfying account of the origin of the universe, our planet, life and the birth of humanity is essential if we are to feel significant, secure, relaxed and happy with our lives; if we are to derive and renew daily a sense of enthusiasm and purpose. Where different stories appear contradictory, it is worth finding common threads in the interests of personal satisfaction and freedom from doubt, and in the cause of global harmony.

Stories about how the world was created

The Genesis story in the Bible tells of the creation of the world by God in six days (and the creation of rest on the seventh). I was told it when I was young and I was also given to understand that this was a poetic vision, rather than the literal truth, so it has never bothered me unduly that this account has been contradicted by scientific observations. Here is part of it:

> In the beginning, when God began to create the universe, the earth was formless and desolate. The raging ocean that covered everything was engulfed in total darkness, and a breath from God was moving over the water. Then God commanded, 'Let there be light' – and there was light. God was pleased with what he saw. Then he separated the light from the darkness, and he named the light 'Day' and the darkness 'Night'. Evening passed and morning came – that was the first day.[15]

There are parallel stories from different traditions, equally poetic in style (also accepted as fact by many). Here is an example with some similar images. It is Taoist from the fourth century BC, recorded by Chuang Tsu, a man from the Honan Province of China. I like it because it takes human beings and their wisdom into account as well as the simple appearance of matter. It is rather beautiful and retains a complete sense of mystery.

> Among the ancients, knowledge was very deep. What is meant by deep? It reached back to the time when nothing existed. It was so deep, so complete, that nothing could be added to it.
> There is a beginning. There is no beginning of that beginning. There is no beginning of that no beginning of beginning. There is something. There is nothing. There is

---

15 *Genesis*, Chapter 1, verses 1 – 5.

something before the beginning of something and nothing, and something before that. Suddenly there is something and nothing.

The ruler of the South Sea was called Light; the ruler of the North Sea, Darkness; and the ruler of the Middle Kingdom, Primal Chaos. From time to time, Light and Darkness met one another in the kingdom of Primal Chaos, who made them welcome. Light and Darkness wanted to repay the king's kindness and said, 'All men have seven openings with which they see, hear, eat and breathe, but Primal Chaos has none. Let us try to give him some.' So every day they bored one hole, and on the seventh day, Primal Chaos died.[16]

This, according to Taoist tradition, was the birth of order within the universe. At school, I was taught about Charles Darwin and Gregor Mendel, about evolution theory and genetics. These ideas also amazed me, and still amaze me; but instead of providing all the answers, they seem to deepen the mystery.

A more recent version: the Big Bang

The Big Bang theory of the origin of the universe came next. Proposed about fifty years ago, it was verified by astronomical observations in the 1990s. According to this recent version of genesis, the 'Big Bang' happened ten to fifteen billion years ago. To refer to it as 'big' is misleading, because there can be no comparison. It was and continues to be everything that was, is and

---

[16] From *Inner Chapters* by Chuang Tsu, translated by Gia-Fu Feng and Jane English. See 'Recommended Books and Websites'.

will happen. The universe is a totality.

It is also misleading to call the original event a bang, because it was not exactly an explosion. To think of empty space and then an explosion occurring within it, as if a bomb or land mine were detonated at a safe distance, gives a false idea. It is not correct to say that things started expanding, but rather *the whole thing* started expanding. There was nothing else. The Big Bang was the origin of energy and matter, also of space and time.

The origin of the universe must therefore remain somewhat mysterious to us. We have no way of knowing what exactly took place or how it came about. Because we were physically created, and that from which we were created was itself physically created, within space-time, we are conditioned to consider everything in terms of these physical dimensions; but we cannot stand outside them. There can be no such thing as an objective view or version of events. No account of ours can do justice to whatever the Big Bang might have been, or what – if anything – can be said to have caused or preceded it. A degree of humility is required, and this is important when it comes to contemplating our own significance in the context of the whole.

Like the other stories in this chapter, then, we may use the Big Bang to derive meaning and significance, but are wise to acknowledge its metaphorical aspects. It was like a big bang, but it was not a big bang. It was different in essence, and differs therefore in its consequences for us. It works poetically, but becomes problematic if we take this or any other account to be either literally true or complete. The poetic vision can be reconciled with earlier accounts of creation, and many will find comfort in that.

Let's try and make a comparison.

Time, space and matter

According to modern physics, time has everything to do with matter, specifically with the movement of matter through space. We determine a year according to the time it takes planet earth to complete an orbit around our star, the sun; and a day lasts as long as the earth takes to complete a single rotation on its own axis. We then designate equal divisions of this day as hours, minutes and seconds. We measure these according to the regular motion of a dial around the face of a clock or watch, or by the structured movement of numerical images through digital technology.

Time also particularly has to do with the steady expansion of the universe from soon after that initial moment when everything was squeezed into a singularity. It is not possible to be quite sure what happened in the first millisecond, partly because as well as being hot, the matter in the infinitesimal speck was packed extremely tightly together. However, according to this amazing story, our entire universe has confidently been traced closely back to a few seconds after its initiation. It was then composed of a gas under extreme pressure that started off very hot, hotter than it is now in the centre of a star like the sun.

The first stable substance, formed in a matter of milliseconds, was hydrogen. Hydrogen has the simplest and lightest of atomic structures, its atomic nucleus consisting of a single proton.

By about one second, the temperature was about three billion degrees and sufficient expansion had occurred for the particle density to be reduced. Deuterium (known as 'heavy hydrogen', its nucleus containing one proton and one neutron) also Helium (with two protons and two neutrons) began appearing.

At just over three minutes, in the region of 23 per cent of the new matter formed was already helium.[17] All the elements in the periodic table – carbon, nitrogen, oxygen, sodium, calcium, sulphur, iron, mercury, gold, silicon, neon and the rest – have been formed, wherever they exist in the universe, from combinations of hydrogen and helium.

From the first creation of helium, for about 300,000 years, the universe was nothing but a gaseous fireball, growing in size at the speed of light, becoming progressively cooler and reducing in density. As it cooled, it gradually became very dark.

It is difficult to comprehend this account of the birth of the universe when you first hear it. Whatever we may have encountered and experienced ourselves could bear only a feeble resemblance to the actual unfolding of these events. A good way is to deal with it is as narrative – *as a story* – because it is hard to avoid being amazed and awestruck by the details. Also, we are wise to think carefully about displacing earlier narratives completely. They tend to fulfil important needs, other than those of providing certainty or verifiability. They can still help us find a sense of meaning in existence and purpose in life. They can add to a special and valuable sense of belonging. They contribute to a profound sense of well-being, and can be thought of as having spiritual (if not scientific) credibility.

---

[17] Astronomers have discovered that no star, galaxy or nebula in the universe has a lower percentage of helium. This is one of several observations attesting to the uniformity of our universe.

We may do best to think of our new scientific version as a helpful addition to earlier myths and stories. Like them, it is a story which answers some questions but not others. Mechanistic explanations about 'how' do not address the hugely relevant 'why' questions – questions about meaning, about the purpose of the universe's existence, about the creation of life and the place of humankind. These are the spiritual questions. We can examine them cognitively, logically and philosophically, but we should pay attention as well to the important role and impact of our emotions.

We will each naturally have some kind of emotional reaction to this new scientific legend about the origins of our cosmos, especially when we first hear about it. Perhaps we react differently each time we hear it: with doubt at first, with fascination or surprise and wonder, with a measure of anxiety or alternatively with consummate satisfaction, depending on a number of factors. It is quite possible to react to it too with indifference or even boredom.

So far, we have told only the beginning of the modern, scientific tale of our universe. How did the Big Bang lead eventually to our planet's creation, and so to the origin of life and the arrival of humankind? In the next chapters, we will look at the stories we tell ourselves about this, and reflect upon how they might help us feel loved, happy and whole.

Reflections

What would you say to an intelligent child about the origins of the universe and the earth?

8. The Divine Whole

For many people, the importance of the various stories about the origins of the universe, the earth, life and human existence is not some kind of objective, scientifically verifiable truth but something much more subjective and personal. It has to do with wanting to know and be sure that we matter. In particular, we want to know that we do not have to endure lives of suffering for no reason. We want to feel significant, and to find ways of making our own unique contribution. No one likes to think, at the end, that their life has been lived to no useful purpose.

It helps if we can think of the universe as benign and working in our favour. It is better if we can discover intelligence behind it, and better still when we experience a personal connection to that intelligence.

Divine inclusiveness

When we refer to the supreme deity as 'God' we are personifying that from which we take and acknowledge our origins. This is psychologically sound, and allows us to elaborate the nature of the relationship as intimate (using words like 'Father') and respectfully obedient (using words like 'Lord').

The word 'God' stems from the same word as 'good'. According to the Genesis story, then, the creator is good; but this immediately gives us a problem. When we think of something good, we can also think of its opposite quality. If some things are good, it is logical that other things will be bad . . . or evil. This way of thinking depends on our dualistic, everyday minds. While we need to be able to think like this, it does not apply to everything. It does not work with the indivisible. We are wise when we consider the situation using the 'both/and', rather than 'either/or' style of thinking.

According to 'both/and' thinking, then, the divine necessarily causes and contains both good and evil. This seems like a riddle, and a scary one if we want to consider the universe as benign towards us. God is no longer to be associated with just the good. In this scheme of things, God is the author of both the good and the bad.

To take it further, *He* is not only masculine (yang), but also feminine (yin). It is both *He* and *She*, at once and forever. Indeed, we must consider and reflect upon all opposites being contained within the divine whole. Opposites depend upon each other. They are inter-related and constantly interacting dynamically, like the principles of yin and yang. This single idea has far-reaching consequences for how we perceive and interact with the universe, for our philosophy and behaviour.

This unified view is not new; we know this because it has been incorporated into several ancient and related middle-eastern languages. The word for God or the divine in Aramaic, the language Jesus spoke, for example, is 'Alaha'. This is directly related or equivalent to the Arabic word 'Allah', and to the Hebrew word 'Elohim'. All three can be translated best by phrases such as 'sacred unity', 'the all', and, 'the one without opposites'. [18]

---

[18] More information about the broader meanings of Jesus' use of Aramaic words is available in *The Hidden Gospel: decoding the spiritual message of the Aramaic Jesus* by Neil Douglas-Klotz. (See 'Recommended Books and Websites'.)

To discover the true significance of the two ways of thinking about creation involves mental work and a certain amount of reflection. How can we reconcile a unified and benevolent creation with the simultaneous existence of both good and bad? We will need to consider again what we know, and the stories we are telling about what we know, with fresh minds. It is not easy to set aside preconceived ideas, but we do not have to entirely. If we are open to new ideas in the 'both/and' sense, we will surely be able to make progress.

The important question to revisit, then, is, 'Can we count on a benevolent reality?' To put it slightly differently, 'Could we experience the universe as loving?'

A loving universe

In approaching this big question, we should first think about what the word 'love' really means. We are used to thinking in terms of possession and ownership. We love people, property, activities and so on that we think of as somehow 'ours'. However, we will see in later chapters that possessive love (and especially sexual love) is natural early in our journey towards maturity in love, but that mature love is selfless. It is neither sexualized nor possessive. Eventually, as we pass from adolescence and mature through the conformist and individual stages of development to be explained later, we outgrow the kind of love that is based on attachment.

One description of love might be that it involves a feeling that you are an immensely special part of something or someone, and that the thing or person is equally an integral part of yourself. The connection is experienced as whole and intimate. It is thus a 'non-dualistic' experience; one that fills the mind. There is no sense of separateness or separation from the beloved person or object, so you do not feel any need to grasp and hold onto what you love. There is security in this sensation. You do not feel at risk of losing the love and the feeling of love, even if separated from the person or thing that you love. It is like carrying around the focus of your love in your heart. Whoever or whatever is loved fills your being, and fills your emotions with joy, inner peace and contentment. From it you may also derive a profound sense of being esteemed and valued.

Viktor Frankl, referring to his young wife, from whom he was separated in the concentration camps, wrote:

Love goes very far beyond the physical person of the beloved. It finds its deepest meaning in his (or her) spiritual being, his inner self. Whether or not he is actually present, whether or not he is still alive at all, ceases somehow to be of importance." [19]

I was to discover this myself, when I came to solve my Grandfather's riddle, as you will see in later chapters. It may be, however, that few people experience this loving link, this kind of mystical connection "that goes beyond the physical person" in a way that connects you to the entire universe. It is possible, though, even if we are more accustomed to considering whatever is outside our planet and solar system as both cold and remote.

---

[19] In *Man's Search for Meaning*, pp49-50. (See 'Recommended Books and Websites'.)

Our intelligently-designed universe

The way to approach the situation may be from the other direction. It may help to look for evidence that the universe treats us as special. The father in the Upanishads story, for example, might find ways of explaining this to his son. He could try and tell him persuasively about some aspects of physics, and how this is known both to be constant throughout the universe, also incredibly finely tuned to permit life on earth.

The child would learn about gravity from objects falling to the ground, and could be told how amazingly feeble it is when compared with the other forces that affect atoms. Nevertheless, it holds the moon and planets in their courses, and allows us to stay on the ground and to move around freely. If the value or strength of this force were any different – even slightly weaker or stronger – the universe would have expanded differently. We would not be here, because our planet and solar system would not be here.[20]

The earth is said to be about 4 ½ billion years old. Expanding at the speed of light in the preceding 10 billion years, the universe has grown to contain unimaginable numbers of atoms, spread out with an average density of one per every 5 cubic metres of space.

After only half a million years, its temperature was still high (about 3,000 degrees), but it was cool enough for hydrogen and helium atoms to become more stable. The reduction of combustion reactions meant that there was only darkness; a situation that

---

[20] Professor Sir Martin Rees, the current Astronomer Royal, has explained much of this in his popular book, *Just Six Numbers: deep forces that shape the universe*. (See 'Recommended Books and Websites'.)

persisted for hundreds of millions of years.

What might a child make of this? What are we to make of it? The universe seems to have been dark, empty, primitive and lifeless. Who would think that we humans might yet emerge from such conditions? Who can help but be amazed at the immense and precise forces at work over such long periods?

The simple gases in the early universe were not distributed evenly, however. Inside gas clouds, atoms collided with gradually increasing frequency and force. Four hydrogen atoms, merging to form a helium atom, gave off a very specific fraction of their mass as energy: $7/1000^{ths}$. This tiny percentage is then released from the gas cloud in the form of light and hydrogen has become the basic fuel of the stars.

To illustrate, a wise man sat his son in a darkened room for half an hour. Then he got up quietly and lit, one by one, dozens of small candles that he had prepared beforehand. Just imagine how amazed and delighted the young boy was. Just imagine your own reaction, should you have been there after aeons of total darkness, when one by one the earliest and most primitive stars began twinkling in the night sky.

If the fraction was any smaller, hydrogen atoms would never have fused to become helium in the first place. If it were only one-thousandth part larger, all the hydrogen would have combined to become helium early, with none left to power the stars and no prospect of the later formation of water or denser elements. It is comparatively easy to conclude that something very special, and very significant for our eventual existence, was happening according to intelligent cosmic design.

The boy would be told by his father that the stars of the first generation were simple in composition. The fusion of hydrogen and creation of helium within each was time-limited, ending with all the hydrogen being consumed by the process. Gravity causes the exterior parts of these early stars to collapse into their centres, raising the interior temperatures, allowing the heavier helium to become fuel also. More complex nuclear reactions then result in the formation of larger atoms, including carbon, oxygen, magnesium, silicon, sulphur, iron, calcium and so on through the entire periodic table of elements.

As these stars grew older, gravity at their surfaces diminished so they expanded to become 'Red Giants', ten or twenty times larger than our sun. Either their outer layers then dispersed gradually into space, or a stupendous nuclear explosion blasted the star's exterior outwards at great velocity, ten or twelve thousand miles per second. At the time of such an explosion, for a few weeks, the star, now a 'supernova', would have shone thousands of times more brightly than before. Later, the remaining 'neutron star', might only have been twelve miles in diameter, but it would have weighed half as much again as the sun.

These are astonishingly impressive phenomena, but they are more than spectacular cosmic events that continue to occur throughout the universe. Our very existence depends upon them. Our sun, about five billion years old, is a second generation star, formed from the remnants of supernova explosions, as were the congregation of planets – including our own – that came to surround and orbit it. We are made, quite literally, from star-vapour and stardust.

A human-friendly system

The number of atoms in the body of a human being has been calculated. It is very high. A child would have to raise his ten fingers and multiply them more than twenty-eight times to get close to the actual figure. We are a carbon-based life form, heavily dependent on oxygen and hydrogen, for the air we breathe and the water we drink. Iron, abundant in the earth's core and responsible for the earth's magnetism, is an essential component of the molecule haemoglobin in our red blood cells, which captures oxygen from the air in our lungs and carries it to where it is required for energy production throughout the body and brain. Calcium is essential for the formation of bones. These facts have been known for many years, but they are no less amazing for that.

Some people will say that there is nothing to get excited about, however exact and fine-tuned the physics of the universe appears to be. It may not prove that we are special, but the odds against this universe, this planet and these life-forms having come into being are so immeasurably tiny as to be worthy of serious contemplation. A natural response might be humility, wonder and gratitude, and I encourage you to explore your thoughts and especially your feelings in the face of such an apparently coherent and human-friendly design.

This, in my view, is about acknowledging with our whole personalities the great and unified mystery of existence. It is not for us just to think about and decide whether some kind of divine creator has been and continues at work. This leads to an answer that is too simple, one that will be too dependent on 'either/or', dualistic thinking and will easily be capable of dividing people with different beliefs and opinions, leading to opposition and conflict.

In Chuang Tsu's book *Inner Chapters* is written:
Where there is questioning,
There is something beyond the question...
Those who dispute do not see.[21]

This means that if you find yourself in a disagreement with someone, it is wise to look more closely at the subject under discussion. Collect more facts, if possible. Collect more opinions, especially those of recognised authorities, then spend more time in contemplation. Think things through for yourself, from both sides of the argument. So-called 'non-onesidedness' is an important ingredient of wisdom. For instance, did God create all plant and animal life within seven days, or was Darwin correct, and all the different species evolved over a long period of time through the natural selection of random mutations? We are going to examine that next before moving on to consider the complex and personally meaningful realm of psychology.

Reflections

Have you ever experienced any kind of spiritual link to the entire universe, creation or God? What was it like?

How lasting has been the effect upon you?

---

[21] From *Inner Chapters* by Chuang Tsu. See 'Recommended Books and Websites'

9. Maturing Towards our True Nature

Much more than cosmology is tuned so precisely to our existence. There is an abundance of significance to amaze us too, for example, in the physics and chemistry taught in schools. On reflection, it is difficult to avoid feeling immensely valued, and feeling special is part of feeling loved. When we are feeling low and anxious, feeling special and feeling loved helps us to be happy. The type of knowledge – for instance, scientific knowledge – which makes us feel part of something greater is likely to generate curiosity and even passion about similar subjects. Engaging the whole person, not just the intellect, often fuels an enthusiastic lifetime search and with it a career in science.

Reconciling Genesis with modern science

Because of the excellence of my teachers in the field, it was biology rather than the physical sciences that stirred my own first great enthusiasms and decided my fate. Enthusiasm has, quite rightly, to do with being filled by divine energy and purpose. (The '*th*' comes from the Greek word for God: the same as in 'theology'.) In my early teens, I was struck by the energy and amazing fertility, the creative perfection and magnificence of nature, and by its astonishing inter-relatedness. I loved the intelligent beauty of evolution and genetics in combination. It was a joyful day, then, when I was offered a place at Cambridge to read medicine, and I could learn to put what I had studied into a context useful to others.

Scientists and those like me influenced by studying science do well when we remember, and revisit occasionally, the excitement and wonder at the inherent mysteries of the universe that decided and governed the course of our professional lives. For many of us it seems important to retain this kind of grand scale perspective, although some see science and mystery as implacably opposed to one another.

I have never experienced great difficulty in reconciling the Genesis account of creation with that of modern science. The poetic similarities outweigh the apparent contradictions and inconsistencies. We have only to consider the length of a day flexibly and a case can then be made for an acceptable level of compatibility between the seven days (or extended time periods) of biblical creation, on the one hand, and the Big Bang story, followed by fifteen billion years or so of universal expansion, on the other.

A fresh look at creation

This involves only a slight amendment to the way these two stories are told. We could look, for example, at creation like this:

Day One: In the beginning there was the Big Bang, followed by the first fireball (primal chaos)

Day Two: A long period of cooling (darkness)

Day Three: Primary star formation (light), as hydrogen atoms fuse and become helium with the release of energy

Day Four: The destruction of the early stars and the formation of secondary stars from heavier, more complex atoms

Day Five: The addition of planets around the newer stars

Day Six: The emergence on earth of plant and animal life and the eventual arrival of humankind.

Day Seven: This is now. In modern times, the universe proceeds effortlessly to unfold while psychological, social and spiritual development takes place among us here on earth

We will explore the stages of this development in later chapters. Here, we can say simply that through restful contemplation of creation, we are gradually opening up to our wisdom minds, directing awareness towards the sacred perfection of the whole. This is the mentality of the Sabbath day. Increasingly deliberate realignment of consciousness serves to heal and converts all, one by one as individuals, towards maturity.

Human evolution

There is debate about the appearance of humans on earth. Some argue that evolutionary theory, involving the natural selection of random mutations, is a sufficient explanation. For others the idea of randomness is contentious. They postulate as necessary a design engineered by divine intelligence.

To go 'beyond the question' on this matter we need to combine elements of both arguments. It also involves recognizing that evolutionary theory, which began with and works well for biology, is highly speculative when attempts are made to apply it to the complex fields of psychology and sociology.

The key idea underpinning evolutionary theory is that of survival; but this says little to satisfy our powerful need for a sense of meaning and purpose. Survival seems insufficient as a reason for human existence; so, for many people, Darwinism fails to answer satisfactorily the big question, "Why are we here?" A satisfactory answer would benefit all of us but, just as we grow out of childhood stories, we need different answers at different times in our lives. We certainly do not need to agree on a single answer once and for all with everyone else.

Darwin's theory, as far as it goes, can be applied looking backwards to where humans have come from, but is best considered as an incomplete and an allegorical story. It does not give us any reason to avoid or reject a different, possibly complementary story about a cosmically intelligent design.

If we acknowledge God, the Creator, as implied by the Aramaic word 'Alaha' to be a 'sacred unity', it gives us a new and valuable perspective on creation. The design and the designer can be acknowledged as one. Creator and creation are indivisible, a sacred and dynamic unity, an unfolding and divine whole, the purpose of which involves each component being seamlessly connected to and reflecting that whole. As the mystic poet William Blake has it, we may "See a world in a grain of sand/And a heaven in a wild flower/Hold infinity in the palm of your hand/And eternity in an hour".

Sacred Unity

Looking forwards in time, the aim of human evolution from this holistic perspective involves our fragmented, worldly, everyday-minded intelligence growing closer, little by little, to whole, divine wisdom-minded intelligence.

We are designed and destined – both individually and collectively – to be refined in the direction of spiritual awareness, of health, happiness and love. Everything, including adversity, assists us in this.

We partly understand how the biological realm emerged from the physical, and at the same time it seems essentially mysterious. How does that which is lifeless give rise to life: randomly, by design, or both? Next, psychological reality emerged from the biological; minds apparently emerging from evolutionary development of mammalian brains. But how does biology give rise to consciousness: randomly and/or by design?

Both conundrums are examples of yin-yang situations. In each case, two things which are different depend upon each other. One may come first historically; but in this scheme of things, the future may influence the past. If it is my intention to travel by car to Oxford, for example, that I will be there in the future has a direct effect on my actions in the present before I set off. It is about being properly prepared and about finding my way. There is much to think about here.

Human beings are sentient. We have sense perception. We have emotional responses. We can think and act. Not only can we experience, think, feel and act, but we can and must also communicate. We belong in families, communities, cultures and societies. The social dimension thus emerges from the psychological: another yin-yang interaction.

We are going to see that the psychological and social dimensions of human experience make sense best in a spiritual context, in relation to the universal whole. We will concentrate on where both our personal journeys and the evolution of our species are going; on how best to be properly prepared and on finding our way, and on the choices that apparently face us. We will be slightly less interested in where we have already been.

Making a choice

Can we choose what we believe? Here is an opportunity to test that idea. You are invited to pause and consider three choices, in the hope of being able to find a decision.

The first choice is to accept that we humans are special within the universe, to the extent that we are inter-related to it through love.

The supporting arguments include the precision with which the physics and chemistry of the universe have allowed the construction of our planet, preparing the way for the emergence of biology, itself so beautifully and perfectly organized over evolutionary time in our favour, eventually allowing our mental faculties, including intelligence, wisdom, creativity, intuition and the capacity to love to emerge.

The second choice suggests instead that within this universe, given the vast number of galaxies, vaster number of stars and an almost inconceivable number of planets in orbit around them, sentient life forms are certain to exist elsewhere as well. Added to this suggestion might be the idea that our universe is only one of a huge number of universes, each with different properties. Within such a gargantuan 'multiverse', there must statistically be some living creatures comparable to ourselves. According to this second view, we are not special but both accidental and commonplace: there is no design or designer.

The third option is to accept neither of these choices, but simply to weigh them up without coming to a conclusion. This is not an abdication but, if honest, a prudent delay until one feels more certain. "To defer is not to abandon" as the saying goes – and it does seem important that each person comes to a point of view, because the questions amount to this: 'Do I matter or not?' Self-esteem, an important ingredient of happiness, is at stake.

Some people find it hard to argue against the *logic* of the second view, based on scientific theories and observations; but it is easier to argue against the *wisdom* of it. To accept that we are not somehow unique and special is to risk removing a powerful source of meaning and motivation; to do so gratuitously and unnecessarily. A life without meaning or any sense of purpose can easily become one of unremitting misery. Who would wish for that?

Personal growth often depends upon taking control; on making choices, taking responsibility for them, and enduring the consequences, advantageous or otherwise. This is how we grow wiser. There is an obvious link here to courage as well as wisdom. We do best with a spirit of adventure.

When we have developed a degree of maturity, we will be more capable of adopting the 'both/and' style of thinking, instead of 'either/or'. We will start to see validity in both sides of each argument and begin to accept with equanimity that we are *both* special *and* commonplace inhabitants of an unthinkably vast universe (or multiverse).

It is not so important to make one choice, hold onto it defensively and seek to propagate it. It is deep-seated anxiety that makes us grip our choices too tightly. Those who feel anxious in the face of uncertainty, and who are most comfortable with only one – the best or the correct – solution to a question, are still in an adolescent stage. They have yet to mature. This is not criticism, but an aspect of personal development we all have to work our way through.

The wisdom here of 'both/and' thinking involves the freedom it gives, and the possibility of redirecting our attention to what is happening around us. When getting the right and only answer to the question becomes less of an insistent priority, we find from a more detached perspective that there is much to do for our own good, and for the good of others, in the local environment. We find too that we have more energy at our disposal for useful work and it is better to get on with this than spend time on imponderables of little immediate consequence.

Here is another story, told to illustrate the importance of discovering inner conviction, and of making a stand whatever the cost, as part of the process of personal growth. Called 'Barn Burning',[22] it is from a short story by Nobel Prizewinning author William Faulkner. The events are set in the Deep South of America after the Civil War. The central figure is a boy who is not given a

---

[22] Included in the collection 'Faulkner's County'. (See 'Recommended Books and Websites'.)

name. He stands for all of us and is, perhaps, about twelve. He is rapidly about to grow up.

The Barn Burning story

At the outset, the boy's father is in court accused of burning down a barn in angry revenge upon a neighbour. The boy knows that his father will want and expect him to lie, to save him from conviction and punishment. The boy also knows that he will lie if pressed, partly out of fear, however much he obviously dislikes the idea; but in the story the father is released before the critical moment. The boy is temporarily excused from his moral dilemma. The family, however, are forced by the townsfolk to move guiltily on.

The boy feels the hatred of others towards his father, but the father gives him no credit. Sensing his son's turmoil, he turns and accuses him: "You would have told him", meaning the father thought his son would have told the truth to the Justice of the Peace. As a warning the father hits the boy, reminding him that he is getting to be a man. Then, threateningly, he says, "You got to learn to stick to your own blood or you ain't going to have any blood to stick to you".

The man and his family travel on, settling at another spot where there is casual farm work. Again the father embroils himself in a grievance, this time against his landowning employer, whom he eventually sues unreasonably for payment withheld. The father has damaged property of the employer and the suit fails, so the boy knows (and we, the readers know) that the father will take his revenge angrily as before, disregarding the consequences.

The boy is sent to get fuel for starting the fire. When he returns with it, he is weeping. The father makes his mother hold the boy, to prevent him giving a warning, but an aunt speaks up for him and, his mother distracted, he manages to break free, running from the house that his father and older brother had left only moments before.

We understand vividly that the boy is torn between fear, family loyalty, self-interest and the higher motives of fair play, justice and the protection of others. Faulkner brilliantly captures the boy's ambivalence with a phrase. On his way to give the alarm, we read of "The terrific slowness under his running feet". The boy seems to want to run faster, but is delayed by a mysterious kind of reluctance. Eventually, he does reach the house and gives the warning, screaming it out because the barn is already burning. The employer immediately sets off on horseback after the boy's father and brother. Running back again, the boy hears gunshots. He stops, crying, panting and sobbing aloud, "Father!" But his father has been killed. The moment of crisis has arrived.

Courageously, at great cost, this boy has chosen honour and honesty in the face of angry threats and the temptation to collude not only with his father and brother, but with his mother and sisters too. This would have been "sticking to their own blood" as the family tradition and the bullying ways of the father tried to insist. We are reading about a genuinely transformative experience for the boy, whose circumstances have insisted on him making a difficult choice. Now he has to live with the consequences.

Faulkner goes on to describe him sitting at midnight in the aftermath, with his back symbolically toward the family's temporary dwelling place. He sleeps while, in Faulkner's words,

"The slow constellations wheel on". Nothing prevents movement within the cosmos. In the morning, we learn, the boy's breathing is easier. He decides to get up and move on.

The remainder of the story is low-key but triumphant. It ends with the boy, as follows:

> "He got up. He was a little stiff, but walking would cure that too as it would the cold, and soon there would be the sun. He went on down the hill, toward the dark woods within which the liquid silver voices of the birds called unceasing – the rapid and urgent beating of the urgent and quiring (harmonious singing) heart of the late spring night. He did not look back."

Faulkner seems to intend that the boy recognised his kinship with humanity as equal to his kinship with his blood family. This was the transformation, the irreversible step in his psycho-spiritual development, sealed by the events of the few days covered by the story. He may have been terribly young, but he was growing up. Facing an irresistible destiny, he could no longer return to the innocence of childhood and follow his family's direction. He was getting to be a man, his father had told him, and he had been forced to decide for himself how to behave.

The choice, he discovered, rose powerfully up from within. There was really no choice, only that of submission to a kind of spiritual imperative and of following his true nature. His wisdom mind forced itself upon him, we might say. The outcome was bad for his family, but it left the boy calmer, more mature and with a real future – one of freedom, not subjugation.

Many people have found themselves behaving well against their own expectations. They often then find themselves, as a result, both transformed and liberated by the process, breathing more easily, so to speak. Much effort and energy is taken up by ambivalence, by *'the human heart in conflict with itself'* to which Faulkner draws our attention. The same energy is now free for more constructive uses. The path of honesty, of honour, of virtue is simpler, clearer, calmer and ultimately more joyful once self-interest and ambivalence have been set aside. This, as we shall see, describes the path of spiritual growth from conformism and conditioning to emerging individuality and eventual integration with the whole, wherein lies peace.

Reflections

What were your passions in childhood? How have they influenced your adult life?

Do you think it possible that the present is influenced by the future?

The boy should have stood by his family. Equally, the boy had to report his father to the authorities. Have you ever been in a similar bind, involving split loyalties? How was the situation resolved?

10. Transforming Problems of the Human Heart

On accepting the Nobel Prize for Literature in Stockholm on 10 December 1950, William Faulkner said that the only subject matter worth writing about involved 'problems of the human heart in conflict with itself'. Young writers, he said, should leave no room in their workshop for 'anything but the old verities and truths of the heart, the old universal truths of love, honour, pity, pride, compassion and sacrifice'. Faulkner does not exactly call them spiritual truths or values, but that is what they are.

'Man is immortal because he has a soul', Faulkner wrote, 'A spirit capable of compassion and sacrifice and endurance. The poet's, the writer's duty is to write about these things'.[23] A different kind of writer, James Fowler, in *Stages of Faith,*[24] describes his research into how people develop throughout life in terms of spiritual maturity, and we will be looking more closely at this concept in later chapters. First, we will consider the psychological processes involved in transformation and growth from an emotional perspective.

The process of transformation

How we respond to the big questions of life depends where we are

---

[23] Faulkner's Nobel acceptance speech is also published in his book, 'Faulkner's County'. See 'Recommended Books and Websites'.

[24] See 'Recommended Books and Websites'.

on our spiritual journey. To discover inside yourself a powerful force for honesty and good, especially if it takes you by surprise, can set in train the process of transformation.

You might ask yourself, 'Where do these fine impulses come from?' Some will say they come from heaven, from God who is good, recognizing Him as the source of individual goodness and other acclaimed virtues. Others may say that altruism has evolved with humans from earlier primates because it is a successful survival feature; but in the Barn Burning story, the boy put himself at risk by opposing his father and family. It was his *spiritual* survival that seems to have won out over the *physical* survival of his father and the material welfare of his brother, mother, aunt and sisters, left as a result of his actions without their main breadwinner. So the story points to our truest nature being virtuous. This nature belongs to everyone, only we have somehow forgotten it, or have been conditioned against it in everyday life.

Whatever we may think, most important will be the experience itself, that of something very powerful, impossible to resist, taking control. It is not surprising that many people who have experienced it think of this as a 'spiritual' force, because it is mysterious and also absolute. It is devoid of opposites or contradiction. While present, however briefly, it takes over your whole being, redefining your objectives and whatever gives meaning and purpose to your life. The only response is submission, an attitude which defines one of the world's great religions. The word *Islam* translates as 'submission' or, more completely, 'submission to the Will of Allah, God'. Christians will be used to a similar idea which they describe as 'obedience'.

Experiencing spiritual force

During such an experience, no argument can stand against such powerful inclinations. Thought, emotion, speech and action are unified. You can do nothing except act out its imperatives and surrender to the consequences, as did Faulkner's boy. One might not even be aware of the grip of such a force until later, so completely does it dominate consciousness at the time. No 'I', no subjective self, is present to observe the mind driven in this way. Our minds are empty of self at such times, and full of intuitive wisdom, full of the sacred knowledge of that unifying whole with which they are fully, if momentarily, in tune.

This poses problems when we try to understand the psychology involved. If there is no subjective awareness, only God or the universe in control, we cannot recall the exact experience to mind and reproduce it at will, or ask an experimental subject to do so. We can only trace its echo, staying with us and continuing to guide us throughout our lives. But clues are available. We are told that the boy was weeping as he returned with the gasoline for his father to start the barn fire, and that he was crying and sobbing aloud at the moment he realises that his father has been killed. We are told that he is calmer the following morning. His breathing is easier, and the birdsong Faulkner describes seems to reflect the boy's own emerging joy.

Here, then, is a brief account of a substantial *emotional* shift; from utter misery and despair into its antithesis, into the reverse or complementary state of happiness and hope. So, in order to make sense of the psychology of transformation, we can make use of the scheme or checklist of seamlessly interconnected emotions mentioned in Chapter Three.

Painful	Pain-free
Wanting (desire/dislike)	Contentment
Anxiety	Calm
Bewilderment	Clarity
Doubt	Certainty
Anger	Acceptance (non-anger)
Shame	Worthiness
Guilt	Innocence (purity)
Sadness	Joy

It seems to work like this. The boy *wanted* something that he could not have; harmonious relations with his father and family members; while remaining true to his powerful instincts for honesty and decency towards others. He also *wanted to avoid* something he was powerless to prevent: his father's vengeful destructive actions towards his employer's property.

Holding on to this set of incompatible desires and aversions caused his misery, provoking increasingly intense painful emotions among which, reading into the text, Faulkner identifies for us as anxiety (fear), bewilderment, shame, guilt and sadness. The boy cannot see a way out because his brutal and domineering father seems to be in control. However, circumstances intervene twice in the story. Firstly, the Justice of the Peace lets the father go free before the son is called to give evidence against him. This brings temporary relief, but seems ultimately to increase the tension, having crystallized for the boy and his father the conflict between them.

The second crisis, however, does not provide any avenue of escape. The new circumstances serve only to enforce the boy's dilemma. He intuitively feels compelled to act, and in doing so must let go of his conflicting desires. He has to give up both his wish for family harmony, and his wish that his father would change his behaviour for the better. He has to give them up because it is too late now for these options. As a result, the feelings within him have simply become too powerful to be ignored. He is no longer under the control of his father, but neither is he yet in control of himself.

Emotions and spiritual release

As these developments proceed inexorably, there is a great release of emotional energy. The boy weeps, cries out and sobs. Exhausted, he eventually sleeps. On waking, he is calm. Giving up and letting go of all emotional investment in his impossibly incompatible desires, the painful emotions convert spontaneously into their counterparts: sadness to joy, bewilderment to clarity, anxiety to calm and so on, allowing him unfettered now to move on. He has grown up overnight and is liberated, not only from his bullying father but also, more tellingly, from his own powerful but draining desires. He does not yet know clearly what he does want from life. He is momentarily content; but he also is perhaps now aware of a reliable inner guide, and will be better equipped to cope with life's challenges and vicissitudes in future.

In Faulkner's poetic vision, the boy's bridges back to his former way of life are burning, like the barn. Just as the leaf, fallen from the tree, is unable to find its way back again, and as a butterfly emerges irrevocably from the chrysalis, so the boy has become a man who can never return to the more naïve and immature state he has left behind.

This seems to be one of the psychological laws of the universe. We naturally develop desires and attachments, which we later must, or can choose to, relinquish. Emotional energy is freed up and released in a process known as 'catharsis' (from a Greek word meaning 'cleansing'). It can take the painful form of tears, or the happier one of laughter, either way resulting in a feeling of spiritual release and purification brought about by an intense emotional experience. Certainly, these two main types of catharsis – laughter and tears – often herald some form of irreversible transformation and growth.

Let me illustrate this with another true story, from my own psychiatric practice. As I tell it, I will emphasize the emotions experienced at different stages by my patient, June. She was in her mid-fifties when her GP sent her to see me some years ago, and this is what emerged from our interviews.

June's story

June was from a poor background. Her parents were frequently bad-tempered because of this hardship. June was never allowed to ask for anything. Her requests were always rejected. As a child, she was made to help her mother and look after her younger siblings. She was permitted little time to play and develop friendships. Later, her father insisted that she leave school to start earning money for the family. At seventeen she met Ronnie, and eventually agreed to live with him. Ronnie had steady work and the local council eventually provided the couple with a small apartment, so June's life seemed to improve considerably. But Ronnie was possessive. He had a cruel streak and a liking for drink, and he was often unfaithful.

June put up with his violence and inconsiderate behaviour as well as she could, for she was too ashamed to return to her parents and ask for their help. She never cried openly, partly because it was her nature to conceal her feelings, and partly because to do so would have inflamed Ronnie and risk another beating.

June wanted a child, and found she became pregnant easily. She looked forward to having someone to love unconditionally, and someone to love her in return, but she had a disappointing series of early miscarriages. When, after four years with Ronnie, she carried her latest pregnancy into its sixth month, she was delighted, but hardly dared show her feelings for Ronnie was not pleased. He was thinking selfishly about the expense of an extra mouth to feed and one day, after a heavy bout of drinking, he assaulted June so badly that she went into premature labour. At the hospital later they told her that the baby had died. Even then, she suppressed her feelings and did not let herself weep.

When she had some of her strength back, June recognised that she was at a crossroads and decided to leave Ronnie. Without letting him know where she was going, she went to another town and found work there as a chambermaid in a seaside hotel. She was a hard worker and readily volunteered for extra hours. She tried to keep herself to herself, but she was good-looking and men naturally found her attractive. It seemed easier for her to choose one of them to spend time with, in the hope that this would protect her from the attentions of others. June picked Len, who was nineteen, because he seemed gentler than the rest, and was boyishly handsome. Len soon took her to visit his mother.

A widow, Len's mother turned out to be a stern, pinched-face woman who immediately insisted that the couple were formally married. June did not mind the idea as she thought she would be safe with Len, but conflict returned to her life very soon. The better to preserve their small income, the couple went to live with Len's mother, and it was not long before a tug of war broke out between the two women. For June, it was like being back with her own domineering mother. She looked to Len to stand up for her, but he was unwilling or unable to risk upsetting his mother, and this led to arguments between the two of them. June had never argued with a man before. She was surprised how angry she felt, and the strength of it frightened her. Losing her own temper reminded her of Ronnie and his frequent blind rages. She was not only terrified but also ashamed that she might be violent, just as he had been.

June was also surprised by how meekly at first Len took it when she berated him. However, like Ronnie, Len too started to drink excessively. Dampening with alcohol the feelings that arose every day, living with two women who had come to dislike each other so much, was the only way he could cope. When intoxicated, however, he also became increasingly bold and bad-tempered. At such moments, June found her thoughts and emotions begin to freeze. It was like a rerun of her relationship with Ronnie, and brought back many unpleasant memories and powerful fears. In a panic one day, as a reaction to all this anger, not least her own, she escaped. Once more, she simply packed her suitcase and left. Len divorced her later, and she never saw him again.

The next few years were difficult for June. She moved about the country taking jobs where she could, always moving on before getting too settled, before attracting unwanted attention. More or less deliberately taking little trouble with her appearance, she soon lost her sparkling looks. She had a natural sympathy for people, and was generally well-regarded, but she did not let anyone get emotionally close for a very long time.

Things eventually changed for June. In her mid-forties, she went to work in a care home for disabled children, who gradually drew her out of herself. She laughed for the first time in many years at their smiles and their antics. Hers was an infectious, tinkly kind of laugh, and it caught the attention of Sam, a widower with two teenage children, James and Becky, who lived next door to The Lodge. Leaning over the fence one summer afternoon, he started a conversation with June, and they soon became friends.

June liked Sam instantly. She felt sorry for him, especially because his wife had died of cancer seven years earlier, leaving him to bring up the children. But he was a cheerful and uncomplaining man. They began spending more time together. They thought of it as companionship, but soon it grew into love. June found Sam's children loving too, especially Becky. So, when Sam proposed marriage several months after they first met, a little reluctantly she agreed.

June assumed that she would now find it easier to be contented and happy. She expected to feel at peace, so it was a shock that she did not understand when, several months into her new marriage, she began experiencing prolonged fits of crying. She lost much of her energy and drive, had difficulty sleeping and lost her appetite. Saying it was depression, her GP gave her some tablets to take, but June was not satisfied. The pills did not seem to help, so she went back to the doctor for advice, and he recommended a psychiatric opinion.

June did not want to speak to a psychiatrist. 'Surely, I'm not that bad', she thought. But she agreed to come and see me from an innate sense of obedience, and she knew that Sam was worried about her.

I felt sympathetic towards her from the beginning, and this must have conveyed itself to June. It was fairly easy to gain her trust and get her to tell her story. She was bright enough to see where my questions were leading, and to co-operate fully when I probed her feelings as well as the facts. As we reached the end of the first interview session, June repeated her problem. 'I cry. I cry a lot, and I don't know why. I should be happy. I've got everything I always wanted. I've got a loving husband, and his children love me too. We've got a beautiful house, and there are no money worries. It just doesn't make sense. Why do I cry all the time?' It was my turn to do some talking and offer an explanation.

'You are crying now, June,' I told her, 'because you are loved. Sam loves you. Becky and James love you; and because they love you, you are now safe, safe enough to allow yourself to cry.'

This seems to be how our minds work. From childhood, June had suffered many things, and had had many reasons to cry, but she learned to suppress and hold back the tears. She did this automatically, because it usually made things worse if she was seen crying by her parents, by Ronnie or by anyone else. This was part of her conditioning.

I said to her, 'It is as if you have built up a reservoir of tears all this time, a great lake of them; but there is no need to worry. I am sure that you are going to be fine.'

The healing process had begun with her tears. I explained that she was crying for her former self, for the June who had uncaring parents and a bully for a partner, Ronnie, then a weakling for a husband, Len. She closed off her emotions for so many years as a way of protecting herself. This was not deliberate. Her mind did this for her; but the children at The Lodge started to bring her back to life. It was like waking up.

'Sooner or later,' I told June, 'We must all wake up and face the suffering, as well as the happier side of life. Life wasn't necessarily meant to be easy.'

The healing power of painful emotions

It seems to be a rule that painful experiences come so that we can be healed. Winter comes before spring; foul weather before fine. We have to face and actually experience stored-up emotional pain before it will dissipate. When we do, it is the pain that heals us. The pain itself becomes the medicine. It is unpleasant, but it does us good. The tears and pain not only heal the emotional wounds of the past, but also transform us, helping us grow.

Recognising that June was experiencing a profound and prolonged catharsis, I was able to tell her confidently that, when it was over, when all her suffering had been used up, she would be well again and feel renewed.

'Does this make any sense to you?' I asked. 'Yes,' she replied. 'I think so. But how long will it go on for? I am frightened that these tears are never going to end.'

She seemed reassured by the idea that every tear shed was one less in her reservoir of misery, and that she would empty it eventually. I thought it would be days or weeks in her case rather than months or years. 'Coming and talking to me about it will have helped,' I told her. 'And I will see you again regularly until you are better and confident once more.'

I asked her to remember that it is good to cry, even if it feels unpleasant at the time, and reminded her that her life was back on track, that she was no longer adding to her reservoir of distress. We even agreed that she could begin coming off her anti-depressant tablets, because June no longer wanted her painful feelings suppressed chemically, now that she accepted that in her case they were both normal and healthy.

June came to see me again two or three times over the next few weeks. She told me parts of her story in more detail, each time revealing – and relinquishing – something important. Sometimes she did so tearfully, but increasingly as time passed with humour. A couple of months later, June was off medication entirely, and she was happy again.

'I hated my parents for a long time,' she explained. 'I did not even admit to myself how much… But now I just feel sorry for them. They were young and poor, just like Ronnie and me, just like Len and me too. Ronnie wasn't all bad. He had had a rotten time with his father, who was an even bigger drunk and womaniser than

Ronnie. It's in the genes, I suppose. And poor Len! He never got away from his mother's apron strings. Anyway...' she smiled. 'It's water under the bridge now. I just don't feel bad about it any more. It's done, and I feel free to move on in my life with Sam and the children.'

She said she was grateful, and recognised that she had been going through a kind of grief process for her younger self. 'It had to be done,' she said finally. 'I wouldn't want to go through it again, but in a way I am glad that I did. I feel so much better for it in myself.'

Reflections

Have you ever been surprised to discover inside yourself a powerful force for honesty and good?

Are you comfortable with emotions – your own and those of other people? Look at the checklist. Are there some that you are more familiar and comfortable with than others? Some that you particularly seek to avoid?

---

11. The Healing Power of Love

Many of us would benefit from the ability to recognise emotions as they arise moment by moment, but emotions tend to be fleeting, and detailed emotional self-awareness is relatively rare. It is, however, a skill that can be acquired and improved through training and practice.

The checklist of basic or primary emotions is helpful because it is easier to recognize something when you have a name for it and some kind of description. The basic checklist feelings resonate with each other, so the list represents a kind of musical scale (equally a kind of rainbow or spectrum) with two interconnected sides or wings: painful and pain-free.

Four levels of emotion

Different levels of emotion were first described long ago by ancient Greek and early Christian writers. Adapting their ideas, we can say *first* that there is an immediate feeling, such as sadness or joy. The feeling is triggered by noticing something: something within, such as a new thought or memory, or something external, an event of some kind. This is the most fleeting type of emotion.

The *second* level involves background mood, lasting for more than just a few moments. This feeling might be more complex, including several of the primary emotions in the checklist, both painful and pleasurable, for example when you are not sure about an event or experience.

The *third* level refers to a more permanent disposition. It is often easier to spot these things in others. "She is always cheerful", we might observe, or, "He is usually grumpy and resentful". The difference between the second and third levels is partly one of duration. The third level will also reflect something of each individual's personality, but it is still possible for a person of normally happy disposition to suffer a low mood for a period of hours or days.

The *fourth* level of emotion depends more on how we think about ourselves, our overall reaction to our lives as they unfold. "I am happy with it", or, "I am unhappy with it" provide the most general alternatives. We could refer to this as 'social' happiness (or unhappiness), because it involves awareness of other people.

Different kinds of happiness

There are two main and contrasting approaches to finding happiness: comparative and sympathetic. The *comparative* approach involves a more or less permanent sense of competition. According to this, a person's happiness depends on a sense of having more than, or being somehow better than, someone else. It depends on how we think we measure up to others. It is not a very stable or secure form of happiness, being so dependent on getting (or failing to get) results, on success and failure. This is why it may be considered relatively immature. A person using this approach is always at the mercy of life's vicissitudes, instead of being able to ride in a more relaxed way the inevitable ups and downs.

The *sympathetic* approach is comparatively more mature. It comes from seeing the good in others, rejoicing with them in their good fortune; and also in doing good for others. Our happiness using this approach, based on fellow-feeling, compassion and kinship, is more reliable. When problems arise, others are more likely to be sympathetic and help in return. If there is a drawback, it has to do with the risk of exhaustion as we try too hard to help others. This kind of generous attitude needs to be tempered with wisdom, with recognising that we must ensure our own continuing health and emotional stability before we can be of best service to others.

To summarise, the word 'happiness' can be thought of as having four related meanings. Firstly, happiness reflects the immediacy of joy, momentarily filling our minds (throughout this book, 'joy' can be taken to mean happiness of this kind).

Secondly, happiness refers to a more prevailing mood, which usually includes feelings of calm and clarity, the absence of anger or any of the other painful emotions.

Thirdly, happiness relates to a more enduring attitude of placid and joyful contentment or equanimity. The good feelings usually dominate over the bad ones. (I will use the word 'happiness' for both the second and third levels of meaning.)

Fourthly, happiness also refers to the thoughts a person has when reflecting upon his or her life. It is a matter of personal judgement. To be happy with one's life again reflects a degree of contentment.

Finally, there is a *fifth* level of meaning of the word 'happiness'. This is better understood if we use another word – 'bliss'. Bliss, like joy, is immediate and fills conscious awareness, but with great intensity and often for much longer, for minutes or even for days.

It is a rare experience, but an important one to include, because it seems to be profoundly transformative, resetting the emotional mechanism and marking a big step away from the painful towards the pain-free. There is no equivalent sensation for any of the painful emotions.

How emotional healing works

We will return to the subject of bliss later. For now, to clarify how emotions operate on the several levels described, we will look at June's story again. There are three essential observations. Firstly, she had been wounded emotionally, both severely and repeatedly. Secondly, she was healed eventually by the power of love. Thirdly, Sam's healing love was of a mature kind: sympathetic, generous, unconditional, and in no way controlling or possessive.

June's parents may have thought to themselves that they loved their daughter, but they treated her like a possession in their control, almost at times like a slave. June did not experience tolerant affectionate love, and so did not truly come to think of herself as lovable. She had doubts. This explains why she wanted to escape her parents, and why she also wanted a child; someone innocent, someone to love and be loved by unconditionally in return. However, both biology and circumstances were against her. Ronnie too, with little experience of being loved, was unable to pass love on to June. We might speculate on what painful emotions he was suppressing with the help of alcohol; shame and guilt, perhaps, after his outbursts of anger; but I did not meet Ronnie and feel safer speaking of June.

Like many young people, June had a strong image of her future:

one day she would get married and raise children, and she saw herself working, making a modest but definite contribution to her community and those around her. This was her desired future. This was a set of ideas to which, we can say, she was strongly attached.

Emotional pain depends on such attachments. Likes and dislikes, desires and aversions, propel the entire emotional scale into resonance. It works along the following lines.

Objects of our attachment and aversion range from simple physical objects, such as a prized photograph or a precious item of jewellery, to full-blown ideologies encompassed by a word or short phrase such as 'capitalism', 'communism', or 'impressionist painting'.

An attachment can be to anything encompassed by a single thought, any thing (or 'think') we can give a description or name to, whether real or created within our imagination. In the adolescent June's case, we are considering a range of ideas summed up most simply by the phrase, 'her future'.

The moment we want something, we are open to emotional pain of some kind; often, in the first place, *anxiety*. We wonder how to go about getting what we want, and whether or not we will succeed. We ask ourselves whether or not we deserve it, and so begin to feel *doubt*.

June did not get what she wanted for a long time. She was repeatedly exposed to threats, for example from Ronnie, and losses, such as when several pregnancies miscarried. She suffered doubt and *bewilderment* by being unable to explain her misfortune. Blaming herself, she also suffered feelings of *shame* and *guilt*. She was too ashamed to ask her parents for help, for example, when things went badly wrong in her relations with Ronnie.

June said that she did not feel *anger* at this stage. To do so and express it would have put her further at risk if Ronnie had retaliated, so she suppressed it. She also learned to suppress her *sorrow* and tears.

When we cut ourselves, nature heals the trauma. Cuts bleed, then a blood-clot forms, and elements of the body's defensive system get to work to combat the threat of infection. Organisation occurs within the healing wound, and debris is removed. Lost or damaged tissue is replaced or rebuilt. Sometimes a scar is left at the site of the damage, and often the scar is stronger than the tissue it has replaced or reinforced. Emotional healing is no less systematized, and seems to involve the whole spectrum of basic emotions. Like a physical wound, healing proceeds better under certain conditions. Scarring is also reduced.

How healing can be blocked

If a cut is repeatedly traumatized, the edges are irregular and persistently prevented from joining together securely. Healing is both delayed and incomplete. That is why sutures are used. It is also why plaster of Paris is applied to fractured bones. Splinting improves the chances of healing, and prevents misalignment. It is not the doctor who heals. He or she is simply assisting nature in these cases, having learned her ways. A physician's job is to provide the best environment for healing to occur, and it works similarly in cases of psychological distress and trauma. People require protection from further emotional injury, explanations about psychological processes, and emotional support for as long as it takes, permitting them to grieve their losses. Optimal treatment is therefore delivered with tolerance, kindness and respect.

Even when a doctor cleans a wound and puts in faultless sutures, healing may be prevented by other factors. The person may be weak, undernourished or have some other disorder affecting their general health and metabolism, an infection, for example. It may be so, too, in psychological terms. There are many possible hindrances to emotional healing. Some may require specialist intervention, but there is not space to go into detail about that.

June did not heal psychologically for many years. She did begin to actually experience *anger* when she was living unhappily with her husband Len and his mother, but it also made her *anxious*. This is how the healing process can get blocked. One of the painful emotions switches rapidly to another, without the person being able to experience and tolerate it fully. In June's case, anger set up an unacceptable level of fear and anxiety. She could only deal with this painful combination by avoiding the situation.

June left her marriage, and this may have been wise but psychological healing was consequently delayed. For healing to occur, we have to go through the whole range of feelings, so the process was also held back by her avoidance of sadness. It was as if her intuition of wholeness, her wisdom mind, was protecting her, and had somehow shut down her emotions. For a number of years she was relatively emotionally numb. The unfelt emotions would have been almost unbearably painful and intense, so she had no obvious access to them; but this changed when she finally encountered the innocent joy of the residents of The Lodge, and unconditional love from Sam, James and Becky.

Anger arises when we are resisting loss, when we try to maintain our grip on our attachments. Only when we at least begin to accept the possible reality of such a loss, however important the attachment may have been, can we begin to heal. This is why anger is often so particularly destructive. It depends on the persistence of denial.

Letting go of attachment

With time, June let go of her dream future. Reflection over the years on the realities of her life persuaded her to do so, and allowed the strength of her attachment to this set of romantic ideas to die down. Her doubts had given way in the face of incontrovertible evidence that what she had once wanted would not and could no longer happen. With little doubt left in her mind, she had no basis for either anxiety or bewilderment. By the time she had been at The Lodge for several months, June still felt guilty and ashamed when she thought about her past, and there were fleeting stirrings of anger occasionally, but she had also begun to find a considerable degree of level three happiness, of contentment and satisfaction.

Some of the disabled children there had learning difficulties and others were physically impaired in one way or another. June soon noticed that they all had a kind of spontaneity that was rare. They lived in the present moment, reacting emotionally to everything that happened. It was as if the first three levels of emotions ran together. Their moods changed quickly. Fear, anger and sorrow were frequent visitors, but the children could quite easily be comforted back to a baseline of cheerfulness. They were essentially happy people.

June discovered too that they were often intuitively perceptive about how she was feeling. The degree of empathy was so strong with some of the children that they seemed automatically to tune into June and instantly shared her emotions with her. This was disconcerting at first. When she was tired and irritable one day, an eleven-year-old boy called Jason had a temper tantrum. It was not what she wanted to be dealing with at such a time. As she became more frustrated, Jason grew increasingly angry and disobedient. Luckily, June's supervisor was not far away, and was able to contain the situation. Her first step was to ask June to leave the room. Later she gently explained to June the dynamics of her interaction with the boy. "Sometimes the residents here pick up on your feelings. Then they can't help sort of amplifying them and giving them back to you,' she said. "Whenever we have problems, that's usually what's going on. Maybe knowing about it will help you next time."

June learned quickly. It was often enough simply to apologise and explain to one of the residents, "I am having a bad day", especially if she added, "And it is not your fault". This kind of interaction helped June become aware of her emotions to a much greater degree than previously, and to take responsibility for them and the effect they were having on others. She was grateful to the children. Jason became a particular friend. He was perfectly polite to her when they met the day after the incident, and they seemed to have forged through their brief conflict both mutual respect and a firm emotional bond.

Anger turns to sadness

The negative feelings from June's unhappy past did not, however, dissipate entirely. It was as if they had been distilled down the emotional spectrum into sadness over the years. This was the reservoir of emotional pain that I spoke to her about. She was much less angry and ashamed about her life, but instead she was now sad. She was sad especially for her younger self, and for what might have been. Her continuing solitude, coupled with the absence of affection and respect in her life, prevented the emotional healing process from reaching its resolution. The necessary missing ingredient, supplied eventually by Sam, was love.

With Sam's love, as I pointed out to her, June was free to discharge the inner tension resulting from this great build-up of sorrow. It had its release in the catharsis of tears that provided the original reason for her consultation with me. The tears, however, frightened and bewildered June. They made her anxious, and it was her anxiety that brought her to my clinic. There was a remaining danger of her getting trapped in an emotional loop again; not anger and anxiety in repetitive sequence this time, but a continuum of sadness, anxiety, bewilderment and shame.

My job was to explain the emotional healing process, showing June that her tears were both natural and necessary, allaying her anxiety and allowing her bewilderment to resolve. She discovered in the process that she was not blameworthy. She was normal, like everyone else. This explanation had the desired effect of kindling the healing process, allowing it to reach its transformative conclusion.

Resolution and transformation

The resolution of the emotional healing process is transformative because, when energy is released from the painful side of the emotional spectrum, it is naturally re-invested in the pain-free or pleasurable side. There is no bland or neutral position. That would resemble too closely the emotionally numb state that June inhabited for many years, and nature is much kinder to us than that.

To achieve or have restored feelings of joy, self-worth, innocence, calm, confidence and contentment in place of misery is immensely worthwhile, but that is not all. When emotional healing is complete, we will have grown more mature.

A key element in this maturity is the capacity to experience and tolerate *a wider range* of emotions, painful and pain-free, *in greater intensities* than before. It is not just about becoming a happier person. It is also about acquiring a new degree of emotional stability, of equanimity, and the freedom to think, feel, speak and act more spontaneously.

This freedom is the freedom from former attachments, desires and aversions. It is accompanied by the kind of experience that frees us further from future unwise attachments. It gives us a greater capacity consciously to deny our desires, or accede to them with a greater degree of self-awareness and control. This is a real liberation.

In these new circumstances, we are less frightened because, increasingly able to relinquish attachments, we grow subtly more conscious of having less to lose. We become less susceptible to anxieties and fear, and are much less quick to grow angry. Our minds are altogether clearer. We are no longer so interested in self-centredly calculating the likely profits and losses from our proposed actions, and have correspondingly more mental energy for concentration. We are less distractible. We are thus in better control of ourselves.

Being less defensive, we are also naturally experienced by others as more friendly and trustworthy. We have suffered, and so recognize more readily the suffering of others. This makes us not only tolerant but also less competitive and more sympathetic, viewing others in the world with compassion. Everyone benefits when even one person achieves the resolution of their suffering through completion of this natural healing process.

When we meet new people, what do they ask about us? What do we want to know about them? Among the main things we identify ourselves by are our age and gender, where we live, our families, our hobbies and interests, and our work. After this we tend to look for more common ground, because we tend to like people we recognise as being in some way like us. "I like you" often equates with "I am like you". These are the people we naturally feel comfortable with, whose company gives us pleasure rather than stress.

How would it be, though, if we felt this way towards everybody; that we discovered a profound and incontrovertible kinship with everyone, despite many apparent differences? This would be to feel and be motivated by a universal kind of love, a love which accepts people as they are and does not seek to change or control them. Even just a taste of this mature, non-possessive, unconditional love would be worthwhile. It is the same kind of love Sam had for June, but extended to everyone throughout the world. Is it possible that we are all destined to grow in love like this, if not personally then through succeeding generations? Could this be what evolution has in store for the future of mankind? In an age of high powered and sophisticated weaponry and the capacity for so-called 'mutually assured destruction' between hostile parties, it is difficult to see humanity surviving otherwise.

There will be more in later chapters about this. Next, however, we will encounter another illustrative tale of transformation. Mrs Cruikshank was over eighty when I met her, but she was still about to make a big psychological shift. It is obviously never too late.

Reflections

Are you able to identify the main objects of your attachment
– the people, things and ideas most important to you?

Similarly, what are your major dislikes, hates and aversions?

---

12. A Healing in the Sunset of Life

When I was in Sydney, I took over another general practice for a time. My friend Arnold was returning to Britain for a holiday and would be away for several weeks. I was surprised when, on the morning of his departure, he called from the airport about Mrs Cruikshank, whose daughter had telephoned him at home earlier in some distress. Her eighty-year-old mother with widespread cancer was experiencing severe pain.

Arnold suggested arranging Mrs Cruikshank's admission to the local private hospital, which I was soon able to do by telephone. He also suggested I prioritize making her comfortable, as he did not expect her to survive long. Arnold was sure that it would only be days; but when I went to see her the following afternoon, she was surprisingly feisty. She admonished me for admitting her to hospital and about delaying my first visit twenty-four hours. She then immediately demanded to know when I would be sending her home. Mrs Cruikshank was blind because of dense cataracts, so she could not see the look on her daughter's face at that moment. It was a picture of anguish at the possibility of having to care for her mother again. She seemed exhausted, and quite unable to cope any longer with this tough-minded invalid.

In the event I prevaricated, saying I needed to go away and look at her X-rays, but the truth after examining her was already clear. Mrs Cruikshank's body was riddled with malignant tumour. There was even a bone fracture in her right thigh where healthy tissue had been extensively invaded and weakened. I wrote her up for even higher-dose pain-killers and light sedation before leaving.

'When are you coming to see me again, Doctor?' Mrs Cruikshank insisted as I took my departure. 'I want to be back on my feet as quickly as possible.' I promised to return again soon.

I visited at least twice a week, usually in the evening after surgery. Mrs Cruikshank's unrealistic attitude seemed permanent. She was always polite, but there was no mistaking the chiding I was getting for failing to cure her quickly and let her go home. Eventually, though, she developed pneumonia. I expected her to succumb rapidly, but again I was wrong.

Mrs Cruikshank had a fever and a chesty cough when I next examined her, so I decided to meet with her daughter and the ward sister to help decide what to do. We agreed that antibiotics might cure the chest infection but, having no effect on the cancer, could only prolong Mrs Cruikshank's life and her suffering. It was a difficult decision but we were quickly unanimous. No antibiotics would be used.

If I felt any discomfort, it was because I thought Mrs Cruikshank in her denial might have wanted and expected to have her pneumonia treated vigorously. However unlikely it seemed to me, she would still be hoping for a remission of her cancer. She could not take part in the decision-making now, though, because she had already become very drowsy, sleeping much of the day as well as through the night. A few days later, I noticed a railing around her bed. She had become delirious with the fever. "We had to put the sides up," one of the nurses told me, "because she keeps trying to get up out of bed."

The previous night, they even had to tie some bandages around her wrist and attach them loosely to the bed frame. Mrs Cruikshank had climbed over the railings and crashed to the ground. Then she had tried to fight the night staff as they were picking her up and putting her back into bed. No one knew where her strength came from. I spoke to the ward sister who described more symptoms of the delirium. Mrs Cruikshank was having persistent paranoid thoughts and, convinced that the nurses were trying to poison her, would not eat anything. Her fall apparently resulted from trying to make her escape.

'You should hear what she calls us,' the sister added in an amused tone. "She shouts and screams at us sometimes. Her language is terrible too. She also regularly spits out the medicine. We have grown fond of her, but it is a struggle. She's a real battler!"

I felt sure I was detecting real respect in these words. I found myself admiring Mrs Cruikshank too. There was little else to be done for her medically. Nevertheless, I felt that she was teaching me something, something about my inexperience and false expectations, also about how a powerful will can affect the course of an illness.

Partly to support the nurses, I decided next to go and visit her daily. Strangely, no matter how difficult her behaviour had been, or how rude she had been to the nurses, she always seemed to calm down when I was there. I used to just take her hand and speak a few words, often unsure whether she heard or understood me. If she said anything, her words rarely made sense, but she seemed to appreciate my presence. The nurses were pleased too. It gave them a few moments of respite. Recently I read, in a wonderful book by a French psychologist who works with the dying, that instinctively I was probably doing the right thing.[25]

The healing power of a confession

Mrs Cruikshank was not only surviving longer than expected but, little by little, she also began to recover from the pneumonia. This was amazing. Even without antibiotic treatment and in its utterly debilitated condition, her body fought off the infection. The fever finally left and her breathing became easier. One of the nurses telephoned me during morning surgery to report the situation, and that evening I found my patient sitting quietly in her bed (with no railings) propped against the pillows, asleep but visibly better and calmer. I remember even now the brilliant sunset, visible through the window, as I sat beside Mrs Cruikshank in the small, darkening room. I took her hand as usual and, a few moments later, she awoke.

"Is that you, Doctor?" She said, turning her face towards me as if she could see with her blind eyes. Saying hello to confirm my presence, I felt that she was looking directly into my heart.

'You know, Doctor,' she spoke slowly, holding my hand tight. "I'm afraid."

That was all she said: 'I'm afraid.' But it was like a confession. It seemed to me like the confession of someone whose life had been full of struggle, but someone whose way of coping had always been to deny her fear, to deny even the possibility of fear. This was

---

[25] The book by Marie de Hennezel is called *Intimate Death: How the Dying Teach us How to Live.* See 'Recommended Books and Websites'.

where her strength came from, a reservoir of buried fear. Weakened by illness, facing death, it finally seemed possible for her to acknowledge her perfectly natural sense of dread; but Mrs Cruikshank was still worried that to others this might appear shameful.

"I understand," I replied. It seemed like the right thing to say.

"Do you, Doctor?" She seemed relieved. "Do you really?" It was as if I had both validated and condoned her terror. Mrs Cruikshank relaxed back against the pillows. I stayed several minutes longer as the light faded, but neither of us spoke until I took my leave as sundown proceeded into night. All that was required had been said.

The following day was a Saturday. I was not due to visit the hospital. The nurses had my number if I was needed, but it was Monday before I planned to see Mrs Cruikshank again. In the event, an emergency then cropped up to keep me away another day, so I telephoned to enquire about her.

"Oh, she's marvellous!" The ward sister reported in her business-like Scottish accent. "Mrs Cruikshank is completely calm now and a pleasure to nurse. She is eating again – not much, but enough – and she doesn't seem to be in nearly so much pain. In fact, I was going to ask if we could reduce the pain relief and sedation. She doesn't need much at all just now. Her daughter is very pleased. They are getting on better than ever, she says. She thinks there has been a complete change in her mother. She says Mrs Cruikshank is thinking more about other people, and keeps apologizing to everybody for being a nuisance. We are all glad she came through that terrible infection. It has been a real transformation."

I was looking forward to my visit the next day. It was also going to be my last in the practice as Arnold had arrived back from England. However, an early phone call from the hospital came as a shock. Mrs Cruikshank had died in the night.

She had lasted for almost six weeks. This had been a remarkable final stage in her life's journey, affecting all in contact with her. I was sad to have missed the chance to bid her farewell, but only briefly. It was a privilege to have been so closely involved.

Our feelings about feelings

Mrs Cruikshank had continued to grow as a person to the end. Her problem throughout a long life had been fear. More than this, it had been the fear of fear. Her pioneer spirit would not allow it, so the problem included the shame she would have felt if she had ever admitted to being afraid. Negative feelings *about* feelings often form the real problem. Feeling bad about feeling bad is what prevents fulfilment of the healing process.

Thinking about her again now, years later, it seems to me that Mrs Cruikshank also had lifelong a negative attitude to pleasurable emotions. She mistrusted them. Whenever she felt calm or joyful, and when she noticed happiness in others too, she immediately became anxious. This is another example of having problematic feelings about feelings – feeling bad about feeling good. Because of her temperament and training, she was not comfortable with joy, and was much more familiar with anger, usually in the form of mild irritation. This negativity was reflected particularly in her relations with her daughter. It was why her daughter never felt that she could satisfy her mother; but she was also unaware that it was not her fault that Mrs Cruikshank seemed so often displeased. Painful feelings and negative attitudes are so easily and automatically passed on from one generation to the next. Discovering them, and importantly making them conscious sympathetically, without adding to the burden, is an important part of the therapeutic recovery process.

Mrs Cruikshank's final illness broke down the barriers of her defences. The cancer weakened her, but it was the fever caused by the pneumonia that resulted in her paranoid delirium. At some level, she must have been aware too of the proximity of death. This was when her suppressed fear came to the surface of consciousness in a confused and all-embracing way. She felt that everyone was her enemy.

A spiritual conversion

When her temperature returned to normal, and with it her senses, Mrs Cruikshank experienced, and wanted to confess, that terrible apprehension. Having done so, she could finally relax. This is what brought on her surprising and most gratifying transformation. When the infection and the fever had passed, she was at last able to acknowledge her fear, and perhaps needed to admit it to someone. She must intuitively have felt that she could trust me to understand and accept her fear without criticism. My acceptance of it as natural allowed her to let go of her coping strategy and her shame. She was finally free of shame and terror both. Liberated, she showed us in her few final days what a mind released from painful emotions is like: at peace, quietly joyful, alert, content and considerate of others. This, for me, was a revelation.

It was, as her daughter later said, a kind of conversion experience, right at the end of her life, not in a particularly religious sense, but certainly a *spiritual* conversion.

Mrs Cruikshank had stuck to her principles all the way through. She had been a devoutly hard working person, strong-minded, serious, and critical of others, especially when they seemed lazy or frivolous. Finally, though, after the fear she experienced had worked on her like a medicine, she became more relaxed, cheerful, tolerant and thoughtful of others. Her daughter said it was as if her soul had been healed. It was not a planned or conscious development, but one that resulted from natural healing processes. At the time, it appeared to us providential: God's grace and mercy at work.

Mrs Cruikshank's final illness and death marked an ending too for those involved with her, but also a new beginning. Her daughter became free of a critical and intolerant parent, enabling her to start with fresh attitudes towards herself and the world, as well as the more obvious fact of having more time for herself and her own family. For me, too, this was a life-altering encounter. I have thought a great deal about those moments when I sat beside Mrs Cruikshank during the sunset as she confessed her great fear. I knew intuitively that my acceptance had made a difference; so I learned that there is a special kind of work to do in medicine, work involving the promotion of emotional healing and personal growth as well as physical cure.

This important episode was a turning-point, shaping and sealing my desire and ambition to continue studying the mind and its workings. I realized that I wanted, perhaps needed, to find out more about the mysterious process I had witnessed. From this moment, I was determined that training in psychiatry would not for me be simply an academic exercise. It was to have the decided purpose of grounding me, if possible, in this very special, helpful and healing kind of knowledge and wisdom, enabling me to share it with others in need. If I had not met Mrs Cruikshank I would not now, more than a quarter-century later, be writing this book; and you, of course, would not be reading it.

Spiritual principles

These events demonstrate a number of principles. I think of them as spiritual principles, because they seem to operate for general human benefit, and to do so universally. They apply generally, but have far-reaching consequences particularly in the field of health care.

The first of these principles is that personal growth often depends on experiencing a period of adversity and distress. Life is a kind of journey in which our natural inclination is to seek to avoid discomfort and suffering, but I have known many patients say, as June did, that although they would not have wished for it, their illness had been a good thing.

People often report that facing great loss, as you do when severely ill, either mentally or physically, has helped them appreciate much more what they have. They say it has helped them in deciding what is important, giving new impetus to their values and priorities. The result is a revitalized sense of meaning and purpose, often accompanied by a renewed sense of belonging within their family and community, but also expanded to include greater humanity. People speak of this as a kind of gift, something that is both precious and durable. It cannot be lost subsequently. No one can take it away.

The second spiritual principle revealed by my encounter with Mrs Cruikshank, already mentioned in chapter 2, is 'reciprocity'. Both giver and receiver of kindness get something out of it. Both benefit in terms of spiritual wealth. This is, I think, the basis of health care work as a vocation or calling. People who seek to become doctors, nurses, social workers, hospital and other medical staff, recognize it intuitively. However, attitude is important. You must treat each one you encounter as a whole person, as a separate individual worthy of respect, and so treat them with compassion and thoughtful benevolence. This is the same whether the one you encounter and engage with is a patient of yours or of someone else, whether he or she is a relative of a patient, and it may be especially true of those you encounter repeatedly, such as colleagues.

Kindness, tolerance, patience, perseverance and honesty: these are among the values – *spiritual* values – to adopt and seek to maintain. These will foster confidence in others. People will naturally and intuitively trust whoever displays them. People will repay respect with respect and affection with affection. It was a good day for me some years later, towards the end of my training in psychiatry, when one of my senior teachers said, "I think you are like me, Larry. You really like your patients." I found that I had to agree. Now, I would use the word 'love'.

Reflections

Does Mrs Cruikshank's story resonate with you in any way?

To what extent are you motivated by fear, for example, or anger? Do you have a disapproving parent to contend with; one whose agenda seeks to dominate your own?

Does Mrs Cruikshank's change in attitude so close to death encourage you to think that life may have a purpose right to the end?

13. Calming the Mind

In the final days of her life, following a kind of spiritual conversion, the mind of Mrs Cruikshank became serenely calm. This kind of emotional stability, grounded in the pain-free side of the emotional spectrum, is reflected in the word 'equanimity'. This quality of equanimity means that we have a high degree of emotional resilience, allowing us consciously to experience and tolerate a great range of emotions, painful as well as pleasurable, sometimes in very forceful intensity. As a result, life takes on more vivid hues. It seems abundant, to hold much more for us. This is conducive to more frequent and longer lasting episodes of happiness, and to greater general contentment. Whether we realize it or not, this is what we are all truly seeking. The phrase I use to encapsulate it is 'emotional maturity'.

Improving our chances of happiness

Everyone wants to be happy. We don't want to wait until our eighties for this kind of joyful contentment and emotional equanimity to arrive, or to endure debilitating final illnesses like those of Mrs Cruikshank. Fortunately, this may not be necessary. There are many ways to improve your chances of happiness and contentment. Perhaps the simplest is regularly to practice calming the mind, and to do so in the disciplined way that is called 'meditation'. As we shall see, meditation helps us heal. In helping us to heal, it also helps us to grow.

Few people would question the value of taking regular exercise.

This is how we achieve and maintain physical health and fitness. Why not apply the same idea to mental health and fitness? In this case relaxation is required, a kind of alert relaxation of the mind, rather than exertion. The effort needed is the effort involved in learning any new skill, the effort of bringing yourself to practice regularly. This does not require an imposed, painfully rigid, institutional or military type of discipline, but an essentially relaxed one. You maintain your meditation practice under your own control, at a level that feels comfortable, bearing in mind that, just as with physical exercises and sporting routines, the more you practice mindfulness, the greater the skill you acquire. Just as a brisk long walk once a week will do something towards keeping our muscles in trim, so will periods of mental stillness from time to time be sufficient to improve and maintain mental wellbeing. Similarly, if we exercise too hard or too frequently, we risk physical injury, and likewise there are risks attached to meditating intensively for too long.

Meditation has three major purposes: to calm the mind, to heal the past, and to access the infinite. Before explaining these points in more detail, here is another true story, an allegory by way of illustration.

Canoeing in Canada

I have known Doug since we were teenagers. One summer in the 1990s, I was invited to join him in Canada for a canoeing expedition. Doug, his two brothers and his brother-in-law took a lake or river trip every year with their sons. This time we had three native-style canoes, and I shared one with Doug and his younger son, Pierre, age seven. We took camping equipment, food and supplies for several days, because our plan was to cover 100 miles of Ontario's Spanish River, which, except at our starting and end points, was inaccessible by road. There were no man-made landings or supply stores. It was a beautiful wilderness area.

I was new to canoeing, but my Canadian friends were experienced. They provided good canoes, maps, enough food, and proper equipment. The weather was fair; and so with Doug's guidance I was soon able to master sufficiently the necessary skills and techniques. Meditation should be like this. Many learn its techniques in the company of others, people who swiftly become spiritual friends and companions, even if you did not know them well before. This is a very deep and rewarding, generous kind of friendship, which tends to get you at least pointed in the right direction... downstream. It is possible to make progress alone, but it may be slow or more limited without proper guidance and friendship, as if you are heading against the current, for example, expecting too much too soon. It is best to find good meditation teachers, to help avoid mistakes and discouragement.

We set off from Toronto for the two hundred mile drive, vehicles heavily laden, and failed to arrive at our launch site until dusk. We had to proceed, though, and get on the water despite the gloom, because we had arranged to have the vans driven to our eventual landing site downstream. The drivers were already waiting. By the time we had unloaded the vans and prepared the canoes, it was dark, but there was nowhere nearby to make camp. We had to set off on the river. As a novice, I found this quite scary.

Fortunately, by torchlight, we found an adequate landing and campsite only a few hundred yards away on the opposite bank. Getting there and setting up proved to be a pretty hectic and fraught business. We were hungry, and had somehow to prepare food. I am not sure how we managed; nevertheless, in the morning we had all slept and were ready to paddle downstream.

During the next four days we worked hard, sometimes paddling for ten hours. We had repeatedly to empty water from the canoes. Frustratingly, we occasionally found ourselves running aground or capsizing. Exhilaratingly, we would shoot the safer rapids, but laboriously had to carry canoes, tents, equipment and supplies around the more hazardous. On our third evening together, Doug was even pulled into the river at the awesome, swift-running, three-tiered 'Graveyard rapids', a place worryingly littered with the wreckage of many boats and canoes. We had camped there and eaten by the fire. Doug went off alone in the dark to the riverbank, and was trying to use the jet of water to clean out one of our food bags when the force of it carried him in head-first. He was sucked right under. He could easily have drowned but, luckily, he bobbed up quite quickly and managed to scramble out. The bag, of course, was never seen again. This was a stark reminder that nature is powerful, and needs always to be respected.

The following day dawned brightly. Doug had been shaken by his near-drowning, but was soon once more in good spirits. By midday, after three and a half days of exertion, we reached the final section of our trip. This is designated on the map as a 'Royal Ride' for canoeists. It is where the water runs swiftly and smooth through a long, straight, rock-sided channel. It did indeed prove to be a royal ride. On this final stretch we effortlessly doubled our previous speed, covering the final twenty miles in a couple of hours, reaching our destination – and the vans – on schedule. Three of the men in the group were due back at work the following day.

Canoeing and meditation practice

For many people, meditation practice goes something like this canoe trip. You start barely prepared and more or less in the dark. There are obstacles and difficulties at the beginning, interspersed with exhilarating high points and breakthroughs. Later, your technique and skills improving, what seemed against you now turns mightily in your favour. The struggle abates. The flow is smooth. You are on a royal ride. This is why perseverance is recommended. Often when things seem to be going badly, you will actually be making good progress. There is no easy way of judging your development as a meditator because of this. It is important to accept that sometimes the flow dwindles or backs up, just like water in a river. It is necessary simply to stay afloat.

The allegorical comparison between my canoe trip and meditation can be extended further. The water in the Spanish River has fallen as rain on some of the oldest rocks of the Earth's crust, beautiful, glacier-sculptured pink granite. It flows in streams through dense spruce and pine forests alive with moose, bears, wolves, eagles, chipmunks and butterflies, before joining beaver and trout on the banks and in the river.

Several timescales are represented here: those of the rocks, of the trees, of the animals, of me and my friends (the canoeists), of me now (the writer) bringing together into the present, using my mind and imagination, these different aspects of the past. Now you, the reader – at a different time – are doing the same, building up a picture of that place and the events I have been describing. This kind of seamless and interdependent continuity reflects a powerful truth about existence. It is not fragmented. It is whole. This is the nature of perfection.

The Spanish River flows on still. It flows beyond where we left it at the end of the Royal Ride into a sequence of lakes, eventually through a dam, from which it provides power and electricity for the far-off city of Toronto. The water continues into Lake Huron, over Niagara Falls, into Lake Ontario, then the St Lawrence River, and so to the Atlantic Ocean from where it evaporates, falling as rain again: an endless cycle.

When we are proficient, meditation helps us recognise that the activity of our minds is continuous and seamless too. In meditation, we gradually become aware that there is no 'external' and 'internal', only mind and mindfulness. Everyday experience is not like this. During wakefulness, our minds are dynamically engaged. Our emotions are active. Our thoughts chatter away. Our bodies are frequently restless. The motor is running. The gears are engaged and we are in motion.

In meditation, it is different. There are various techniques with the same aim: to leave the motor of conscious awareness running gently, while disengaging the drive. We are wide awake, but still... and usually silent.

Techniques help focus the mind

There are times, especially for beginners, when being still is difficult, so there are also meditation techniques involving rhythmical and repetitive activity, useful when either restlessness, on the one hand, or drowsiness and fatigue, on the other, render stillness either intolerable or conducive only to sleeping. The simplest of these is walking meditation, which involves walking barefoot up and down for about twenty paces, or walking in a circle. You are not trying to get anywhere. You are aiming to focus your mind wholly on what you are doing: walking slowly, taking deliberate steps, and so feeling the full sensation of your feet striking, caressing and leaving the ground in turn, left and right, over and over again.

Many people discover a healthy form of meditation for themselves, through knitting, for example, chanting or jogging. These rhythmical activities give the mind a focus. Concentration on this focus, light but persevering, protects the mind from distraction. This is the essential feature and product of meditation: a calm and undistracted mind. Everything follows from that.

All the main techniques prescribe a reliable focus of concentration. This might be the inward and outward movement and sound of the breath, for example, a sound or short phrase (known as a 'mantra') to be repeated over and over in the silence of one's thoughts, or a vivid visual image.

To use another allegory, imagine a beautiful, tall sailing ship running smoothly before the wind across a clear ocean beneath untroubled blue skies. Perched on top of the highest mast is a seabird, a gull. Sitting in meditation, let the masthead represent your chosen focus. The gull represents the centre point of your awareness. For the moment the two are together, but the gull soon flies off, attracted by sense perceptions, emotions, thoughts and impulses. Your mind, distracted, has split into two. The yacht with its masthead furrows on straight ahead through the ocean while the seagull flies hither and thither. This is usually the case when someone begins meditation training. It is difficult to keep your concentration focused, but there is good news. The seagull must eventually return to the masthead. The ocean is enormous, and the bird has nowhere to go, nowhere else to land and be at rest. Even on the most difficult of days, if we persevere, it becomes possible to bring our concentration gently back, time and again if necessary, to its original focus, the one we have chosen.

This focus becomes our still-point, our refuge. The word 'mantra' means 'mind-protector'. The chosen word or phrase usually has sacred significance, as may do the images employed in visual techniques. When focused in meditation, our minds are protected from distraction. They are no longer split. The everyday mind dissolves into the wholeness and perfection of the wisdom mind. The two coalesce, blending into one. The ego-mind of desire and aversion is pacified, allowing the more mature mind of the true self to dominate. For the moment, at least, we are unified. We are completely at one, both within ourselves and with the universe. This is the mentality of the Sabbath Day, the day of rest. All barriers and boundaries have dissolved.

Many of the various meditation techniques require bodily stillness, and so the learning of a stable and relaxed posture, usually sitting, comfortable enough to adopt the pose for twenty minutes or much longer, but not so comfortable that you risk falling asleep. Some people find it helpful to count their breaths as they do this, counting each in-breath to four, then starting at one again, to avoid being distracted by counting large numbers.

Benefits of meditation

People who meditate regularly, it turns out, do not require as much sleep as they did before starting their practice. Why is meditation better than sleep? Why might even people who sleep well benefit from meditation? It is about unification and wholeness, and it seems to be connected with being both relaxed and awake, maintaining concentration. It is about observing, but without asserting excessive control over mental content.

The everyday environment at home and in the workplace is seldom calm or free of demands. Life generally either seems too busy, or it feels dull, repetitive and boring. Our ego-minds are capricious, easily swayed from moment to moment by attachment, by desires and aversions. They are like 'monkey-minds', swinging restlessly from tree to tree, forever fleeing discomfort to pursue excitement, novelty and momentary pleasures.

Even when things are relatively quiet, we usually experience dialogue, a conversation with ourselves, inside our heads. It can be experienced whenever we happen to tune in to it. Our ego-minds cannot stay focused. They are on many things at many levels at once, jumping about from moment to moment, at the mercy of multiple needs and desires, our priorities changing all the time. Our minds, fractured and fragmented, no longer seem whole. Our emotions seem to be in control. They no longer remain pristine and innocent, but are readily tarnished with emotions like doubt and uncertainty, by shame, guilt and remorse. We are no longer mentally and emotionally clear, but become clouded by confusion, bewilderment. We no longer experience utter calm, but grow easily troubled by anger and discontent. Joy is lost and sadness remains in its place. We may not even know that we are suffering and in pain, and that we long to be healed. If we do know, we may not know the extent of it. Meditation, however, can set us on the right path.

When someone tries to sit quietly and calmly for twenty minutes or so for the first time, it is often difficult. This is because thoughts, words, sense perceptions and impulses crowd in. These seem like distractions from the process of meditation, but it is valuable to pay attention and notice what is happening.

This is your starting point. If your mind is dull and empty, or if it is full and over-excited, your task is to observe and accept what is there. This may seem unnatural, even unpleasant initially. This is so for two reasons. Firstly, we are used to being in control, and feel more comfortable that way; so it can be a shock to realize for the first time that our minds control us, rather than the other way around. Meditation practice will help us regain control, but it cannot be done by simple exertion of willpower and determination. This is usually counter-productive. Secondly, we are all likely to have suffered emotional traumas, both in childhood and later. Unless we have been lucky enough to find love and healing, we will continue to carry the pain of these wounds locked away. As we begin to meditate, so will this pain be released. We have to face and go through it. The pain itself is our medicine.

In order to face this pain, we need a good degree of meditative stability. This is the first step. The longer you sit, and the more often you practice meditation, the more readily the mind will be inclined to settle and grow calm. That is when you will start feeling in control once more. The process is like shaking up a glass of freshly prepared juice. At first, our minds appear cloudy and obscure, like the liquid, but the longer you wait, the clearer they become. Eventually, as the sediment comes to rest at the bottom of the glass, the liquid above it is revealed to be crystal clear. So it is with the mind in meditation. Its true nature is revealed as luminous, full of clarity, acquiescence, calm, joy and delight. It is good to get a glimpse of this from time to time.

The experience of bliss, even if brief, is transformative. It is part of the healing process. The sediment largely comprises the emotional pain we have been carrying, based on our multiple attachments. Some of it, even if only a little, will be dissolved away by the joyful calm encountered when you practice sitting, walking or some other form of meditation.

When the distractions, the thoughts, feelings, impulses and sense perceptions, diminish sufficiently, the diamond-clear wisdom mind is revealed. This is not much of a mystery, because calm and turbulence are natural opposites which complement each other, like yin and yang. Remove one and the other has to appear. Nevertheless, if you have not experienced this degree of mental clarity, it is an exceptional feeling at first. I first experienced it under instruction from an American who was a Buddhist monk, in a group of about fifteen people during the period of my training as a psychiatrist in Australia. It was a complete revelation.

Bringing the mind home

I had helped to arrange a weekend workshop on Jungian psychology. The Jungian therapist brought the monk. We had not been informed that this was planned, and were not expecting it. When the monk was introduced, he simply asked us to put our notebooks and pens away, sit up with a straight back, rest our hands comfortably on top of our thighs, half-close our eyes, and pay attention to the breath as it passed through our nostrils.

'Just focus on your breath,' he said. 'Keep your mind on either the in-breath or the out-breath. Do not worry if you become distracted. It is not a test to pass or fail. Simply return your mind to the breath whenever this happens.' Time passed, perhaps about twenty minutes, although the period seemed quite timeless. Then the monk told us that we could open our eyes.

I can still bring vividly to mind the room we were sitting in together that late afternoon over twenty-five years ago. The stillness was remarkable. The usual chatter inside my head had disappeared. The only sounds came from a small flock of Australian bell-birds in the trees outside, beautiful, clear, lilting calls that seemed to penetrate not only our ears but also our whole beings. These amazing sounds filled our minds to the exclusion of all else. It was a truly mindful experience, and it was like hearing birdsong properly for the first time.

I recall that we all looked around rather shyly then, seeing each other properly too as if for the first time. Every face wore a smile. It was a remarkable moment. Like Faulkner's boy in the Barn Burning story, I was hearing 'the liquid silver voices of the quiring birds' at a turning point in my life.

'Meditation,' said the monk, 'is just this.' He paused to let the words sink in. 'You can think of it as bringing the mind home.' He left another long pause. 'Practice it when you can.'

Another meditation teacher, Sogyal Rinpoche, in his book *The Tibetan Book of Living and Dying* called meditation 'the greatest gift you can give yourself in this life.' From my personal experience, and for reasons that I will explain, I am inclined to agree.

Reflection

What is the greatest gift you have given yourself in this life so far?

---

14. The Need for Love

One of the three main inter-related purposes of meditation involves healing the past. It is not too fanciful to say that the origin of pain is birth. Babies and infants cry. Children cry. We all cry. We have all known both physical and emotional pain from the outset. It does not necessarily result in lasting harm, but most of us carry some echoes of early losses.

One of the causes of emotional pain is to want something that is not forthcoming: comfort, food, relief from soiled baby-garments or whatever. In earliest childhood, we are reliant on mothers and mother figures for our needs and desires. What we need most is love, both to experience love and through it to experience ourselves as lovable. Veronica's story shows that compromise over this can be hard to accept and often has enduring consequences.

Veronica's Story

I left Sydney after about a year. I returned briefly to England, but soon decided to return to Australia and continue training to become a psychiatrist. I eventually found myself in South Australia, and spent three years based at a psychiatric hospital in Adelaide. One day, I was allocated a new patient. This was Veronica. She had been admitted to a general hospital after taking a near-fatal overdose of pills, and transferred to our unit when she recovered from the worst of the physical effects.

It was my job to interview Veronica and discover her story, but she was still feeling sick and had a headache when I went to see her on the first day, and was not ready to talk. I decided to introduce myself briefly, then leave. It helped to establish a therapeutic bond, I think, that, like me, she was English. Trust between us was necessary if we were to work successfully together. I did not want to antagonize her at this first encounter. I said I would return the next day and hoped she would be feeling better.

Unlike most of the overdose cases I had dealt with, Veronica was not an adolescent or young adult. She was a married woman with two school-age children. She had not tried to kill herself on impulse. She had made up her mind to succeed. According to a nurse who had spoken to her, Veronica was still determined to die. When I first saw her, though, she was too weak even to get out of bed.

The next day she looked better and seemed fairly happy to talk. She told me that her husband and children were about two hundred and fifty miles away, living in Mildura. She did not want them informed of her whereabouts, or of what she had done. She said that she had come to town on the overnight bus, checking into a cheap hotel with the deliberate intention of taking her life and dying in anonymity. I tried not to show my reaction, but I was shocked at the strength and single-mindedness of her resolve. I wondered what had upset her life so badly that she wanted summarily to end it. She said she could not explain. Veronica did not want to say much more then, but she did agree not to leave the hospital or to try to kill herself again before I returned the following day.

Within a few days, she was well enough to leave the hospital and travel. Our conversations were beginning to develop, however, and I thought she might agree to stay on for a short while. We needed time if we were going to help make any lasting difference. Veronica was already less intent on suicide, but not ready to face the consequences of her actions leading up to the events I have described. She had allowed us to inform her husband, Barry, of her whereabouts. (It turned out that the police had also been in touch with him after he reported her missing.) Veronica then telephoned him for a short conversation. The future of their marriage was obviously very uncertain. Barry wanted to come and collect Veronica but could not get time off work, or arrange for someone to look after their children, for several days.

This was good, because it meant that Veronica could stay with us longer. I was relatively inexperienced at the time, and was not sure how to proceed, but my handling of the case was being supervised, and my supervisor recommended that I simply make myself available to Veronica for a conversation every day. He thought she would eventually trust me enough, and feel comfortable enough, to begin talking about the causes of her suffering and wish to die. He encouraged me to ask questions, trusting my intuition about what to say and how to say it. My approach should be governed by kindness, and contain no indication of criticism or reproach. The technical term we used then was 'unconditional positive regard', a phrase coined by a leading therapist from the USA, Carl Rogers. Today, I think of it as a mature and selfless form of love. Anyway, the advice was good, and Veronica duly responded.

She told me that she had been born in England towards the end of the Second World War. She was illegitimate; a 'bastard child' as she put it. This was a time when much shame and stigma was involved. Veronica assumed, but was not certain, that her mother had been young and unable to care for her. She harboured a fantasy that her father had been a Canadian or American soldier, but she had no real information about him at all.

Little by little, obviously feeling great shame at what she was revealing, Veronica told me that, from the age of about six months, she was raised in a children's home. She particularly remembered being cold and hungry growing up there. The only way the children could get out was to be fostered into a family. The hope was always that, following a successful foster placement, they would be adopted permanently. Like the other children, Veronica naturally wanted desperately to be wanted, to be loved. She was eventually selected for fostering, but did not prosper in this first family. Other foster children were involved, and none received much affection. She felt that they were set up as rivals against each other. Envy and jealousy frequently gave rise to arguments and aggression. The girls were also treated as unpaid workers around the house. At the age of six or seven, something came over Veronica, as a result of which she rejected the bullying atmosphere and began to challenge her foster mother. She was soon returned to the orphanage, where she was made to look after some of the younger children.

A year or so later, Veronica was fostered again. This time she was alone in the placement, and the parent-figures were kind to her. She was intelligent and did well in her lessons at school, so they were pleased. Veronica felt genuinely warmed by their pride. She began hoping; and soon felt sure that this couple would adopt her as their own daughter. It was wishful thinking, however. There was some discussion about the possibility but the situation changed.

The woman, having thought herself barren, wanted a child and fostered Veronica thinking that this was her only chance at motherhood. When, unexpectedly, she became pregnant, her attitude towards Veronica changed. She no longer wanted her there. Veronica, feeling unfairly displaced in this woman's heart by the new baby-to-be, seems to have reacted angrily once or twice. The woman's husband, who had become quite fond of Veronica, tried to intervene on her behalf with his wife, but as her pregnancy developed towards term, she became implacable. The inevitable result, after less than two years with this family, was Veronica's return to state care.

I am not sure how many times Veronica was fostered into different families, but she never felt accepted, despite trying so hard to please people. She left school at sixteen and found employment, but she remained officially in state care until she was twenty-one, by which time she had met Barry who worked in the same office. They were married on her twenty-first birthday, and decided immediately to emigrate to Australia and begin a new life.

For a time, things went well for Veronica and Barry. The children came along without complication. Veronica found herself capable as a mother, and enjoyed parenthood, but always felt somewhat detached from family life, as though it were not real somehow; that it might suddenly disappear or be taken away. Her first three levels of need were apparently being adequately met, but she still felt that something important was missing. To fill the emptiness, she started to gamble.

It began innocently enough when she was still in England. In pubs, social clubs and other places, in those days, were sixpencein-the-slot gambling machines called 'one-arm bandits' or 'fruit machines'. In Australia, similar devices are called 'poker machines'. Today, they are electronic and sophisticated. Then they were simple. Three in a row of the same fruit – cherries, lemons, pears, bananas – paid out. Three gold bars was the jackpot. If you won, the machine dramatically spilled out sixpences, overflowing into your hands until it was empty. After only one jackpot, Veronica was thoroughly hooked.

I did not ask Veronica to say any more about this when she first mentioned it. Only when I thought about it later did it seem like a clue to understanding her and unlocking her binding to this addiction. Luckily, we had time to meet again before she left to return to Mildura, and she also agreed to continue seeing me at fortnightly intervals, travelling on the overnight bus for a regular appointment until her life had settled once more. Later, together, we worked out that the jackpot win had not been about winning money. It had rather been powerfully symbolic for Veronica, an almost mystical message from her 'Lady Luck' that she had found favour.

This fantasy creation of hers, Lady Luck, was akin to a supremely loving mother-figure who Veronica instantly came to believe in as the silver coins tumbled forth from the inhuman, unforgiving machine. It meant to her somehow that she counted, that she was not condemned to insignificance, to be ignored by life and destiny and fate. So Veronica craved the smile of Lady Luck from that day forward until the craving drove her ultimately to the utter brink of suicide. Winning the jackpot seemed to make up for the many slights and disappointments of her life, for the shame of illegitimacy and an upbringing in an orphanage, for the rejection by one foster family after another. Veronica's rational mind was overwhelmed not by greed for money, but by an insatiable appetite for acceptance and love, as symbolised by further wins on the jackpot machine. Everything in her life was eventually sacrificed to this.

When employed, Veronica had been able to use her own money to gamble. When her children were young, however, she relied on Barry's income. This was adequate, but she felt obliged to keep from him her increasingly frequent expeditions to the pubs and hotels where poker machines could be found. She never varied her gambling. She did not bet on horse-racing, for example. On most occasions, satisfied only with the biggest available win, she would continue playing until her funds ran out. This practice eventually drained the family resources, and Veronica managed, without telling Barry, to raise further funds by re-mortgaging their house. She had forged Barry's signature on the bank documents. With the children both in school by now, she was able to find work and so make up the extra repayments. At first, she also had additional cash to continue gambling.

Lady Luck runs out for Veronica

Eventually, her losses mounting up, Veronica began stealing from her employer. The bank had sent a letter threatening to foreclose on the mortgage as the repayments had fallen significantly behind. Veronica had hidden this from Barry. She had also begun cheating on him with someone she met at the social club where she often went to gamble. She had borrowed money from this man to play the machines. She liked his apparent kindness towards her, but he was soon requesting sexual favours. Veronica was flattered at his interest, and thought no harm would come of the arrangement as long as she kept it a secret from Barry.

Veronica broke down in tears of remorse and despair as she told me how she had so easily fooled herself into thinking that the other man, prepared to lend her money to gamble with, must have loved her as much as her husband did. Barry always argued with her about finances. This had made it easier for her to justify to herself her infidelity. She had given no thought to the effects of all this on her children, assuming that they would never know about it and were not involved. She simply had to have the money. This was her imperative. Once Lady Luck was back on her side, she thought, everything would somehow be fine again. She was, of course, in a state of complete denial.

Finally, the police came to question her about money missing from the accounts at work. She had been altering cheques, making them out to herself. She was not arrested immediately. The police were still gathering information. Her big nightmare was about having to tell Barry what had been happening. This was when she took the overnight bus to the city and checked into the anonymous hotel, planning suicide. She could not face the shameful reality and felt she had no other option.

Veronica's story shows that we each have a deep and powerful need for significance, to feel that somehow our lives matter. We need to feel loved and that in some way we belong. If we do not experience this, the need can emerge pathologically and grow irresistible. With such a powerful drive affecting us, we risk finding ourselves, like Veronica, satisfied prematurely with something destructive. If we accept as our supreme goal something as elusive and transitory as success on a jackpot machine – and many people have such flimsy objectives – then we are equally destined for misery; and we are destined to make misery for those around us, especially those who are closest.

From birth, then, we are subject to suffering, to emotional pain throughout the spectrum, as a result of powerful basic needs, desires and aversions. Life is much easier for those who are – and feel – wanted and loved, and whose needs are provided, but no one escapes bewilderment, anxiety, doubt, anger, shame, guilt or sorrow, because we all have likes and dislikes, preferences and pet hates. The associated pain accumulates. How may we be healed from the past?

Reflection

Put yourself in Veronica's place as you read this story. Reflect on how much parents give their children, and what particular needs they fulfil.

Is there anything in your life comparable to Veronica's reliance on 'Lady Luck'? Is there a mascot that you invoke, for example? Do you have any kind of irrational superstitions at all? If not, do you know anyone like this? What could be missing from a person's life that this attempts to make up for? How successfully does this type of compensation usually work? How reliable is it?

15. Healing the Past

In one of our therapy sessions together, after she had returned home to Mildura, Veronica told me how much she valued the overnight bus journey in each direction. The roads were good and the ride generally smooth. She would sleep some of the time, but also valued the opportunity to calm down and think things through.

I did not know much about meditation in those days, but I am sure now that she will have entered a meditative state for part of each journey. The rhythm of the bus, rolling through the night, would have been conducive to this. Apart from the constant noise of wheels on tarmac, there was little disturbance in the way of sound. Her fellow passengers mostly sat quietly or slept. It was dark, so there were few visual distractions. The bus ride may have done as much as the therapy for Veronica.

She told me that, reflecting on her life, she had been experiencing guilt for the first time. Veronica was no stranger to shame, to feeling unworthy, but she had seldom considered any of her own thoughts, words or actions to be wrong. She mentioned, for example, that throughout her teen years she regularly took things from shops with no intention of paying. She did not count this as theft in her own mind, rather as appropriate compensation for being unloved and abandoned, and for the many wrongs done to her from birth. She felt justified in giving herself small treats in this way on a weekly, sometimes more frequent basis.

Her shoplifting behaviour abated considerably after she won that first jackpot, but the psychology transferred itself to her gambling. Veronica felt she was owed something. Only now in therapy, after nearly committing suicide, did she begin to acknowledge the destructive effects of her behaviour on others, especially on Barry and her innocent children.

Completing an emotional cycle

This change in Veronica supports the idea that emotional healing involves the entire emotional spectrum. Referring to the checklist, if a person habitually avoids any of the eight complementary pain-pleasure combinations, this incompleteness prevents resolution of the process in the face of any loss. That Veronica began to experience and recognize feelings of guilt for the first time, and started allowing these feelings to influence her intentions and actions, demonstrates again that emotional healing leads to psychological growth and also social maturity. The principle of completion is upheld. This is a form of perfection, of making whole. Each ending allows for and heralds a new beginning.

Veronica essentially reached these insights on her own, and polished them during her periods of meditative reflection on the bus journey. When she came for her session, she expressed her new ideas to me. My role was to validate them for her, to confirm that I thought she was on the right track. On the ride home, she would use the thinking time to plan how to explain herself and the changes she was experiencing to Barry, and to plan ways to make amends to him and her children for deceiving them and for risking the stability of the family through her gambling and its consequences. It was not her therapist but her wisdom mind that was leading her.

Discovering our resources through meditation

The three main functions of meditation are inter-related. Calming the mind prepares the way for healing the past. This process is powerfully enabled too by accessing the infinite, by making contact with the primal and absolute source of spiritual wisdom and energy. It is ultimately, too, the most secure source of our happiness. Some would call this process silent prayer, and consider it communing directly with the soul or with God.

The various meditation techniques, in which we concentrate persistently on a given focus, have the effect of calming the mind. The next step, when this occurs consistently during our meditation practice, involves discovering that we have at our disposal the necessary tools for observing and examining the flowing content of consciousness as it arises and disperses. These are powerful tools, as useful in psychology as are microscopes and telescopes in the physical sciences, but they are sadly under-used. It is like having both a floodlight to see the broad extent of our mind's activities during meditation, and a powerful spotlight with which to pick out and examine more carefully certain aspects. Meditation practice helps sharpen and intensify our powers of concentration between meditation sessions as well.

Sitting still and in silence is often difficult at the beginning. This is when you first become aware how distractible your mind is. Perhaps you develop an ache in your back or knees, for example, and with it an impulse to move, to stretch a little; or you may become aware of all the others things you could be doing, more urgent seeming or pleasurable things. You may grow drowsy. This is the time to persevere. You may start feeling anxious that you are not doing the meditation properly, or that you are wasting your time. These are normal experiences, simply to be observed rather than acted upon. It is acceptable to move gently into a more comfortable posture when pain and stiffness arise, but it is best to do so mindfully – that is, deliberately and while paying full attention to the impulses, actions and sensations involved.

If you do persevere, you will soon notice things changing. Other thoughts and feelings arise. This is how healing begins.

After the Jung workshop at which the Buddhist monk taught us his method, I started to meditate regularly every day. This was fairly automatic. Once you begin, the teachers say, you can rely on the wisdom mind to guide your meditation for you. Enthusiasm for the practice and a gentle kind of discipline towards it arise spontaneously. Soon afterwards, in a meditation session at home, the image of a seated black cat emerged in my mind.

A healing story about a black cat

I had been allergic to cats since childhood. Contact with them made me sneeze, made my eyes itch and made me breathless with asthma. The reaction could be quite severe, so I tended to avoid these animals. I even discovered once at a circus that I was powerfully allergic to lions and other big cats.

There did not at first seem to be any particular emotion associated with the black cat image but suddenly then, in the meditation, I became momentarily overwhelmed with a pure and poignant feeling of sadness. My eyes prickled with tears. I was able to notice what was happening, but without my meditation being disturbed. It was happening to me, and I was also present as observer. Within a few seconds, the sensation and the image faded away, but the memory of them was still strong when I opened my eyes about ten minutes later.

As I reflected on what had happened, I suddenly remembered our family cat. I could not think of his name and recalled only that he had been black. I do not recall being particularly fond of him, but he was a perpetual silent presence in the new house we moved to as a family when I was about six years old. He was just always there. I went to a boarding school when I was eight, and it took me some time to realise on a visit home, perhaps a year or so later, that the cat was no longer around. When I asked, my parents told me in a matter of fact way that he had become very ill with some kind of lung disease. The vet had decided to end his suffering by ending his life.

I have no memories of further discussion or any emotional reaction on my part; but I did subsequently develop my allergy. Now, in the stability of meditation so many years later, I seem to have remembered the lost cat and experienced the sadness of grief. It was a very brief experience but a pure and intense one, and it was healing. My allergy did not disappear altogether, but since then my symptoms have been triggered much less frequently, and are milder when they do happen.

After this, I revisited other losses and causes of grief both during meditation and more voluntarily during wakefulness. My tears seem to come much more readily than before, and they are welcome. I have begun feeling good about feeling bad. I am no longer afraid of sorrow overtaking me because, however intense it should be, I know that it will not last and will leave me calmer, freer, more emotionally aware and resilient. Healing and happiness are linked in this way, and the starting point in my case was a boy's natural love for the family cat.

Love involves the deepest and most complete form of attachment. This is what is meant by 'identification'. Like Kelly *identifying* with her pregnancy, as described in chapter 1, I too had identified with the family cat, to the extent that its being was part of my being. After its death, I carried on without acknowledging any loss.

A psychotherapist would say that there were a number of other losses, those involved with going away to school, for example, impacting on me at that time, and that the loss of the cat symbolised much more than the death of a pet. It would not be appropriate to dissect this out too deeply here, but it is right to acknowledge that something apparently trivial can have far-reaching psychological and somatic implications and consequences. The benefit of what happened in meditation when the image of the cat appeared should not be underestimated.

It seems likely that meditation will work in the same way for everyone else. When the techniques are mastered, the mind eventually grows calm, stable and undistracted. The powerful, self-seeking, everyday 'ego-mind' depends for its existence on attachments and aversions. In meditation, these are naturally loosened. The split, ambivalent *ego-mind* gives way, gradually transformed into the whole, universal and selfless condition of the *wisdom mind*. When attachments and aversions lose their power, energy invested in them is loosened and released. That energy surfaces in consciousness as pure emotion. Spontaneously letting go of my attachment to the cat allowed sadness to enter and momentarily fill my mind.

The process of liberating emotional energy

As I am describing it here, the process is gentle. The loosening of attachment and the freeing of emotions can be referred to by the Greek word for loosening – 'lysis'. In cases of more powerful and spectacular change, usually where more complicated emotions, especially contrasting emotions, are involved, we speak of a crisis. When emotion is released spontaneously and dramatically, involving the eruption usually of either laughter or tears, sometimes both, the cleansing process is called 'catharsis'. Lysis and catharsis go together.

When there is an emotional crisis, it is as if a decision must be made for resolution to occur. The Greek word 'krisis' originally meant 'decision'. As healing proceeds and the crisis resolves, the important decision is somehow made. It will be a renunciation, a decision to let something go, to relinquish some form of attachment or aversion. Veronica, for example, gave up her attachment to gambling. She made a firm decision to stop playing the jackpot machines. As she described it, she no longer wanted to. It was as if, in her unconscious mind, the decision had already been made. She had only to accept the wisdom of it, submit and honour it.

What we cry about first, we may come to laugh over later. This depends on maturity, on gaining a measure of detachment and wisdom. Because of the universality of suffering and emotional pain, we observe that life was clearly not meant to be easy. Pain arrives first, before relief, joy, calm and contentment; but we are wise to think often of the transformative potential of emotional pain and the healing process, to reflect on the possibility of calm from anxiety, joy from sorrow and so on. Happiness, smiles and laughter come from the healthy resolution of both our fears and our tears. We will come back to this point again in later chapters. Now, for a more complete understanding of meditation, in addition to the psychological, we will examine what is going on in dimensions not yet considered, at the biological and spiritual levels.

The biology of mindfulness involves the seamless interaction between brain and body, functioning as a single unit. During meditation the brain settles into so-called 'alpha rhythm', according to the measurement of electrical brain activity through the skull. This regular, relatively slow, wavelike form of electrical activity suggests that the brain itself is operating coherently, as a single unit. We can speculate that the right and left halves or hemispheres of the brain, which seem to act relatively independently during everyday waking consciousness, having several different functions one from the other, communicate more freely during meditation, and come into harmony or balance.[26]

---

[26] After writing this chapter, I came across reference to the work of Robert Monroe that seems to support this idea. Monroe used audio technology to synchronize the brain waves in both hemispheres. The results are described as beneficial in adults with insomnia and depression, and in both hyperactive and autistic children. The research continues.

The healing power of meditation

Emotions and memories are sited in the 'limbic system' of the brain, which is a kind of anatomical circuit. In fact, it is like a conjoined double circuit, like a butterfly with a body and two wings of connections, projecting one into each hemisphere. The central part or body of this double circuit is sited near the so-called 'hypothalamic-pituitary axis' at the base of the brain, linked to it by both nerves and hormones. This is the control centre for relaying messages – especially emotionally charged messages – between the brain and the rest of the body via the hormonal, sympathetic and parasympathetic nervous systems. It is a key regulating structure.

Our attachments and aversions are evidently mediated through nerve links between the limbic system and parts of the frontal lobes of the brain where thinking and planning occur. Activity in the limbic system is reduced during meditation. The fronto-limbic connections are less energized and more relaxed. This change assists both lysis (loosening of attachment) and catharsis (emotional release). The anatomical arrangement of structures thus seems ideally suited to managing the healing process. When nerve pathways are used less, they tend to atrophy. There are likely to be permanent changes in fine structure of the brain as a result of regular meditation practice and following healing episodes. Similarly, frequent use results in enhancement of structures, so there may be growth in right-left hemisphere connections as well.

This biological process then permits the release into calm and clear consciousness of encapsulated, symbolic, emotion-laden memories. These emerging emotions complete the spectrum on the painful side. The final emotion to emerge, once a loss is acknowledged and accepted, is usually sadness, but other strong feelings can equally be involved. It might be guilt as in Veronica's case, or a combination such as fear and shame, as with Mrs Cruikshank. Once the final piece of the emotional jigsaw emerges, healing proceeds. Yin becomes yang, and the painful emotions turn naturally into their complementary pain-free equivalents. Here is the list again:

Painful	Pain-free
Wanting (desire/dislike)	Contentment
Anxiety	Calm
Bewilderment	Clarity
Doubt	Certainty
Anger	Acceptance (non-anger)
Shame	Worthiness
Guilt	Innocence (purity)
Sadness	Joy

The calm mind, especially in meditative tranquillity, has capabilities beyond those of self-healing. These are the 'higher powers' such as creativity and intuition. Such powers may even extend to more extreme and subtle capacities, like the healing of others, telepathy, mind-matter interaction and clairvoyance.

Tuning into the wisdom mind
It is usual to be sceptical about these abilities, but even the relatively limited research that has been done on the power of the

unified mind can be hard to ignore[27]. Even harder to ignore are any personal experiences we may have. People who meditate regularly are more likely than those who do not. To recognize and credit such experiences. They become frequent, and do not seem to require a more detailed explanation than "This is the way things are". It is not about understanding the mystery. It is about living it. Small miracles then appear increasingly commonplace. Similarly, the commonplace appears increasingly miraculous.

It seems unwise to underestimate the capacity and powers of the mind working as a whole, single unit, free of distracting ambivalences created by attachments and desires of the ego-mind. What we seem to have access to in sustained and experienced meditation is the wisdom mind, directly, timelessly and seamlessly connected to the entire wholeness of the universe. What does that feel like? It feels like a breakthrough. It is a "Wow!" experience of pure amazement, but there is more to be said than that.

In the first place, not every such amazement experience will be an authentic breakthrough from mundane to cosmic reality. Secondly, at such moments, the ego is absent. We cannot so much have the experience as the experience somehow has itself through us. This is hard to describe, and perhaps impossible to explain adequately to anyone who has not been through it. Thirdly, though, the breakthrough experience does not last very long. The ego-mind begins to reassert itself within minutes, possibly within seconds. Nevertheless, in authentic cases, this is enough. A transformation

---

[27] See, for example *The Conscious Universe: the scientific truth of psychic phenomena* by Dean Radin. See 'Recommended Books and Websites'.

occurs. You have caught a blissful glimpse of non-duality, of infinity and wholeness at the same time, in other words of perfection. You have felt the inexhaustible energy of the universe, the pure wind, the gentle breath, the loving spirit of the cosmos, and are bound forever to identify with that, rather than anything less complete, rather than with anything petty, parochial or partisan. You may acknowledge it as a blessing; for, in this life-changing moment, you will have found and become your true self.

The full-on experience may be rare, but every meditation session permits resonance with it, allowing us to be affected by a powerful echo of the true self, and this in itself is healing and promotes maturity. The divine echo is always there for us to access and encounter. In this, it is like the ever-present background radiation of the Big Bang. Once we know how, we can tune in whenever we want.

Remember the description of the Spanish River, originating as rainfall on ancient granite, flowing on and on to the ocean before the water evaporates to fall again as rain in an endless cycle. This description demonstrates how the future, as well as the past, may have a place in the present moment. There is a clue here too about how joy and wisdom are to be found in meditation. When boundaries and barriers like those between past, present and future are not so much broken down as seen through, the true and seamless nature of reality can be first glimpsed, then gradually seen more clearly and eventually grasped.

This is the wisdom that comes when, following spiritual breakthrough, everything is witnessed as an integral part of everything else. Simply being with yourself, bringing the mind home through meditation, allows boundaries, obstacles and barriers, including the barriers resulting from perceived differences between yourself and others, to retreat. What comes, if you persevere with meditation, is an attitude of tolerance and acceptance. In this, your greatest gift to yourself turns out to be a gift to many others as well. Rather than feelings of intolerance, anger, frustration and powerlessness, with regular recourse to meditation and the wise acquiescence it fosters, you get joy, contentment, love and a secure peace of mind. There are other spiritual practices which can help, and we will be taking a look at those too.

Reflection

Have you tried meditation? Would you like to catch a blissful glimpse of perfection? Have you yet discovered any aspects of your true self? Think about your potential for doing good in the world, and for avoiding doing any harm.

16. Accessing the Infinite

One of the best books on the biology of spiritual experience is *Zen and the Brain*[28] by James Austin. My friend Jim is an American professor of neurology who became a practitioner of Zen meditation in Japan during the 1970's. Zen is a pared-down form of Buddhism, teaching its adherents to break through from everyday consciousness to ultimate reality through combining two main methods: meditation and the koan. A koan is a kind of riddle with no obvious solution. One of the best known is "What is the sound of one hand?"[29]

Systems of education throughout the world rely on 'either/or', cause and effect thinking, and are aimed at promoting our powers of logical reasoning. We are often then confronted with choices over 'correct' or 'incorrect' answers. This is the essence of dualistic thinking, and those who are successful academically usually excel at this essentially competitive approach. We are trained to be ambitious and to form an immensely strong attachment to success, to winning, to 'getting it right' and 'being the best'. This gives us a sense of the flawless type of perfection, rather than ideas of wholeness and completion. The problem with someone winning is that, at the same time, other people are losing. This system necessarily results in emotional pain.

---

[28] See 'Recommended Books and Websites'.

[29] Some people know this as, "What is the sound of one hand clapping?" But, with one hand, there is no clapping, and all the more to make us think.

Logical thinking gets in the way of trying to 'solve' a Zen koan. This is exactly the style of thinking that the koan is designed to shatter, because it prevents access to truth at a deeper level, to the ultimate truth of the universe.

Understanding riddles

Koan-like puzzles may occur to us at any time, although we do not often see them as opportunities to break through the tyranny of logical thought. We just feel bewildered, even ashamed at our inability to make progress with them and usually give up. Persistence, however, is one of the qualities required to penetrate these riddles and benefit from them.

Perhaps the most profound such riddle we can ask ourselves would be "who am I?" What comes to mind first when you ask yourself this question? For many it will be their name, so we ask again, "Who were you before you had a name?" "What if your name had been different, taken from another culture, for example?" The real question to emerge will be along the lines of "Who is your true self?"

The characteristic of a koan is that every answer you think of can lead to another question, increasingly hard to penetrate each time. Sometimes, though, you may feel you just have to continue wrestling with it, until you find a satisfactory endpoint at which all the questions are answered and a sense of contentment supervenes. It is not about intellectual ability, but about natural wisdom.

There is a sense in which it is also about having faith that there is another level of understanding to be discovered. This faith gives you the confidence to persevere, and may be a source of much-needed patience.

Pontius Pilate set a kind of koan when he asked Jesus, "What is truth?" and Christians are set many other spiritual riddles by Jesus' life and teachings. How can a man be born of a virgin? How can he die by crucifixion and come alive again on the third day? How can the one God also be three: the Holy Trinity of Father, Son and Spirit? There are no logical answers here; so where do we go, how do we make progress?

The koan and relationship

The tradition in Zen Buddhism is for the koan to be set for the pupil by the teacher. They meet regularly. The teacher has only become a teacher after going through the process satisfactorily with his/her teacher, and he with his. These teachers can trace their lineage back centuries to great Zen teachers from antiquity.

The pupil is given a koan to study only after demonstrating certain personal qualities and attaining a satisfactory proficiency in meditation. This is because constancy of effort is required and meditation provides the tools necessary to penetrate the riddle, the ability to observe the contents of one's mind as with both a floodlight and a searchlight. There are descriptions of people wrestling with koans who experience intense extremes of emotion during the process. Frustration is common, but all manner of other feelings and associated memories may emerge. It becomes a very personal exercise. One person's experience of "The sound of one hand" will be unique.

One common factor, though, is the relationship with the teacher. In cases where the training works out, and the koan is to be useful, the nature of this relationship will be one of mutual devotion. Some would call it a relationship of selfless love. This key factor is often overlooked by those sceptical of the value of Zen tradition and practice. In order to penetrate the mystery of the true nature of reality, we need to experience unconditional love. Similarly, when we do experience love, we will be experiencing the true nature of reality. I suspect that when a breakthrough occurs, the pupil simultaneously recognizes his or her true place in the heart and mind of the teacher. To experience yourself as the subject of another's veneration while thinking yourself all along as wholly unworthy is likely to be transformative. This is especially so when the person is someone you have long revered yourself.

Similarly, when a religious person experiences divine love, beliefs about a Supreme Being or about God, whatever religious, agnostic or atheistic tradition you adhere to, are less important than having this profound spiritual experience and connection with the cosmic whole.

Jesus spoke often of love and said that the nature of God is love. In the context of a spiritual breakthrough, you feel amazed, humbled and blessed. That the supreme totality of the universe should accept you too as whole, just as you are, strikes you deeply. We can refer to this type of transformation as a spiritual conversion.

The bond between a person and God, the totality, is in the form of that seamless type of identification we call love, and as such it extends in both directions. Whoever feels loved by the one true God of the Universe naturally comes to love this sacred unity in return.

Remember, in middle-eastern languages, the words for God

(Alaha, Elohim and Allah) mean just this: 'Sacred Unity'. It is not a question of belief, but one of experience. It is an experience that changes the nature of a person's understanding of both God and the universe. It is an experience of completion, of wholeness, of indivisibility between oneself and the universe. In a way, that is all. Such a conversion does not necessarily feel like a conventional religious experience. It has nothing to do with this religion or that religion. It involves a connecting principle between all religions and none. As a result, it is possible to try and live a holy life without going to a church, a mosque, a synagogue or a temple. As humanity begins to leave secularism behind and enters a post-secular era, that is what many people are already turning towards.

In the Zen tradition, when a breakthrough in which a person's everyday dualistic or logical thought patterns are silenced and the greater, unified wholeness is suddenly glimpsed, it is referred to as 'kensho'. Jim Austin has told me about his own kensho experience, and describes it in his book.

At 9.00 am on a March day in London in the early 1980s, Jim is on a railway platform waiting for a train to Victoria. He is going to a Zen session led by his teacher. It is Sunday and peaceful. He recalls idly surveying a relatively uninspiring scene southwards in the direction of the River Thames, when:

Instantly, the entire view acquires three qualities: Absolute Reality; Intrinsic Rightness; Ultimate Perfection. With no transition, it is all complete. Every detail of the entire scene in front is registered, integrated, and found wholly satisfying, all in itself.

Jim then describes a second wave of insights:

> This is the eternal state of affairs. It has always been just this way, remains just so, and will continue just so indefinitely.

> There is nothing more to do. This train station, in and of itself, and the whole rest of this world are already totally complete and intrinsically valid. They require no further intervention.

> There is nothing whatsoever to fear. [30]

Only five to ten seconds have elapsed since the onset of this experience. Next, Jim describes first becoming aware that this new view of things is too extraordinary to be conveyed; second that he cannot take himself so seriously any longer; and third that he feels somehow detached or distant from outside events.

He feels completely released mentally and especially good inside, both revitalized and enormously grateful. He is clear that the experience is an objective one, lacking all subjective ties and attachments. As he gets on his train, moments later:

> The feeling is of being awed, deepened, and calmed within a profound ongoing intellectual illumination.

You will not meet a more sober and retiring man than Jim Austin. He was already fairly mature in years when these events occurred.

---

[30] Zen and the Brain, pp 537-9

176
LOVE, HEALING AND HAPPINESS

This is not an account born of self-aggrandisement, but one to be trusted and valued. Jim's experience was primarily visual. The scene conveyed a sense of being:

> Viewed directly with all the cool, clinical detachment of a mirror as it witnesses a landscape bathed in moonlight.

People have described similar breakthrough experiences triggered by other sensory experiences – sounds, for example – and by particularly significant ideas or thoughts arising spontaneously. There is also a physical equivalent, brought on by some kind of perfect action of body and mind acting as one. A well-known book, *Zen in the Art of Archery* by Eugen Herrigel[31] describes this.

It seems that for a true breakthrough to occur, a person requires preparation, either by life's events or through previous tuition. Jim Austin was so prepared by his Zen training. The remainder of us, unprepared and unprovoked, can still experience the perfection of momentary ego-absence, even if it does not amount to a complete breakthrough. It once happened to me like this.

Zen Golf

I was about twenty years old, a keen but only middle-handicap golfer. On a warm, sunny July Saturday, I took part in a club competition. There was a big entry. We played in groups of four, and progress around the course was slow. Arriving on the tee of a short hole, my playing partners and I discovered three other groups

[31] See 'Recommended Books and Websites'.

already waiting. It was a question of trying to be patient.

I can still picture the scene in my mind as we waited, mainly in silence. There wasn't much breeze, and the situation was conducive to reverie, even trance. Perhaps I went into a kind of meditation because, when it was finally my turn to play after about thirty minutes, I was operating on autopilot and I hit a perfect two-iron shot, two hundred and five yards right into the hole.

It was strangely as if someone else had done it. My mind had taken control of my body without me. I barely felt that I deserved the congratulations I received from all around me. It was a wonderful experience, but not in the way you might think. It was humbling. Briefly, like Jim on that railway platform, I felt awed, grateful and strangely calmed.

This hole-in-one experience helped me later to understand authors like Herrigel and Sekida[32] describing the aim of Zen practice, to allow the ego-mind to settle, and the wisdom mind in permanent and seamless connection with the totality of the universe to run the show.

Perhaps this set me off on my search for my true or original self, but on that day, the magical moment over, I recall growing excited and distracted. I finished the round poorly, eager only to get back to the clubhouse, tell my friends what I had done and begin the celebrations. Perhaps it changed me, in the sense that a seed regarding the possibility of perfection had been sown in my mind, but it did not immediately change me very much. Later in life, I

---

[32] Katsuki Sekida, author of *Zen Training: Methods and Philosophy*. See 'Recommended Books and Websites'.

learned to take this mystical kind of experience more seriously, whether it was a personal one or involved somebody else. In South Australia, about a year before meeting the Buddhist monk and learning how to meditate, I met a woman with clairvoyant powers who seemed spiritually connected; and she had a message for me.

Meeting Mrs Woodcock

Mrs Woodcock was a widow in her seventies, living alone in a large, well-appointed house in the rural outskirts of the city. I was introduced to her by a friend. We visited only once. On that occasion Mrs Woodcock gave us afternoon tea. She seemed reserved and very British, so I was intrigued when, as we were sitting there, she said she wanted to ask me a personal question. She wondered if I minded.

By way of explanation, Mrs Woodcock told me that she and her husband had come from England many years earlier to study the aboriginal people of South Australia. Professor Woodcock had been an anthropologist. Mrs Woodcock was his assistant. The native Australians had befriended them, and the Woodcocks had mounted many long expeditions into the outback to live with and study them. As they gained the confidence of one particular tribe, Professor Woodcock had been invited to go through some of the male initiation rites. His wife was later welcomed by the females as one of the tribe too, and underwent the female initiation rites in her turn.

She did not describe or explain these to me, but she did say that through them she had spontaneously developed certain powers of clairvoyance, and retained them ever since. She had been advised that these were a by-product of the initiation practices, and that she should not be distracted by them. Sometimes they might be useful, but for the most part, they were safe to ignore. This fits with the teachings of other traditions, like Tibetan Buddhism, regarding telepathy, mind-matter interaction (moving objects, switching machines on and off at a distance and so on) and other capabilities arising from intense meditation practice.

In this case, though, Mrs Woodcock wanted to share a clairvoyant experience with me because it was puzzling her. She told me that she had a mental image of me as an infant sitting on the knee of an older man who was showing me or allowing me to play with his golden watch chain. There was, however, no watch.

'He was very important to you, that man,' she said. 'Was he a relative?' I had to say that I had no idea who he was. Several weeks later, however, on a holiday visit back to England, I took my mother and grandmother for a drive and told them about Mrs Woodcock's question. My mother could not say who the man might have been, but my grandmother instantly piped up from the back seat. "That was your grandfather", she said. "He never did get a watch for that chain!"

My grandfather had died fifteen months earlier, and his last words to me on the day he died had been, "See you in four years.' I was still trying to work out what he meant. In particular, I began to worry that I too was going to die at the end of the four-year peri-od – and I was still only in my twenties. Mrs Woodcock's clairvoyant vision was going to galvanize me into some serious reflection on the subject of death and dying.

Reflections

What is the nature of the devotion between valued pupil and revered teacher? Have you known such a relationship? (For example with an uncle or grandparent, not necessarily an official teacher.) If so, think about this person and what they have given you.

Will you soon be ready to pass on what you have gained?

17. Facing Death

You do not have to belong to or practice a religion to live a holy life. You do not have to be well educated. You need only to be regularly and consciously connected to the infinite, the source of cosmic energy, wisdom and love. For many, the hidden saints of our communities, this happens naturally. For others, life events and circumstances play a part.

My Grandad's Story

My grandfather, George Old, was born in 1906. Even my grand-mother knew little about his early life, and he never spoke of it; but his family were poor, and he left school early to begin work. He remained a building site labourer until illness prevented him from working when he was in his late fifties. I was about thirteen when 'Grandad', as we called him, had the first of a series of strokes. He was paralysed down the left side. In due course, he was unable to walk and confined to a wheelchair.

Before this, I remember him as a humble, shy and taciturn but cheerful man. From my grandmother's stories, I know that he was capable of passion, but this would be in private. In public, even at family gatherings, he seldom showed strong emotion.

By the time I first went overseas in 1975, Grandad had been sitting in his wheelchair for twelve years, doing little but watch television and read undemanding cowboy novels. He had a lot of time to sit quietly and think, and perhaps commune with his soul. Circumstances were forcing meditative reflection upon him. He grew no more talkative, but I am sure that he did grow significantly wiser and more loving.

While I was away on the other side of the world, my mother wrote a letter to say that Grandad's health was deteriorating. She knew that I was due to return for Christmas 1976 and said, "I think he is hanging on to life until you get back. He wants to see you again."

I arrived back on Christmas Eve that year, and was due to remain in England for only four weeks before returning south to Australia. When I immediately visited my grandparents, I found Grandad very weak and barely conscious. His voice was surprisingly soft and husky. He was taken into hospital soon afterwards, but I was off around the country to visit other family members and go to a friend's wedding. When I saw Grandad again about a week later, he was looking much better. He was still in hospital, but alert and smiling. He was also quick to introduce me, his grandson, to the ward sister as a doctor. Apparently impressed, she invited me into the ward office as I was leaving. There was something the medical team wanted to share with me.

At this point I thought Grandad had a chest infection which was responding to antibiotics; hence the improvement. This was true, but it was only part of the story. When the young ward doctor arrived to talk to me, he said little but simply put up an X-ray, somewhat brutally, inviting me to look. It showed that my grandfather had an inoperable grapefruit-sized lung tumour in the middle of his chest, close to his heart. Because the tumour had damaged the laryngeal nerve, which controls the voice-box, I should have made the diagnosis myself from his husky voice. However, in the circumstances, I was a grandson. I was not thinking like a doctor at all.

It fell to me to telephone my mother with the sad news that Grandad was not expected to live very long, and she in turn told my grandmother. We agreed not to mention this to George, as advised by the hospital staff. This was common practice then, although I would recommend only openness and complete honesty now. Grandad was so cheerful whenever we visited. It did not seem right to burden him with bad news. It turns out, however, that he was already aware of his predicament, and seemed to welcome it.

A few days after the news of his cancer was given to us, I took my grandmother to see Grandad in the hospital. It was mid-January, but the sky was blue and the sun shining. The day-room on the ground floor at the end of the ward where they sat was warm and pleasant. I left them alone for an hour to give them some privacy. On my return, the long-married couple were clearly at peace with the silence that had descended over them. I sat down. Grandad was smiling, as usual.

"What are you thinking about, George?" My grandmother asked him. "Six bits of wood!" He replied quickly with a lopsided grin.

I don't think she understood, and it took me a moment to realize that he was referring to his coffin. It still seems amazing to me how cheerful he was. I was a little embarrassed, feeling caught out because we were not being honest with him about his illness. A little later, two nurses came and took Grandad back into the ward, helping him into bed again in preparation for the arrival of the evening meal.

Outside, it was already quite dark. When he was settled, my

grandmother and I went over to say our goodbyes. I remember the twinkle in Grandad's eyes as I shook his hand, leaned over and kissed his cheek.

"See you in four years!" He said to me.

"But I'm coming to see you again tomorrow, Grandad,' I replied.

He was grinning, and simply held up his good hand with four fingers outstretched. My grandmother said her goodbyes and kissed him too. When I looked back from the door, he was still smiling, and again held his four fingers aloft. He died about two hours later.

We held Grandad's cremation ceremony a week later, the day before my flight to Sydney. I made light of his comment about seeing me in four years when I told my mother about it. She suggested that he was just confused, not realizing that I was due to visit him again before flying off. She did not think that he could have known how close to dying he was.

At the time, I preferred not to think about it. I had plenty to occupy me with a new life in Australia beckoning. Later, though, I began to wonder. The meeting with Mrs Woodcock made me reflect on all this again.

I would say now that my grandfather had become like a Zen Master. Through hours of sitting in silent reflection, connected directly to the mysterious infinite, he knew things without knowing how he knew them, and would sometimes say things without knowing exactly why he was saying them, confident only that they were right in the circumstances. This surprising utterance, "See you in four years", was perfect for the moment, perfect in the sense that it prefigured completion. Let me try to explain.

Letting Go

After Mrs Woodcock's reminder of a profound, cosmic link between myself and Grandad; as evidenced by her clairvoyant ability to envision us together, playing with a gold watch chain; I started thinking again about his final message. Was I going to die four years on, in January 1981? If not, what else might he have meant? Despite my clear recollection that Grandad had been cheerful and smiling when he held up his fingers and waved them at me, I could not at first rid myself of foreboding. My death had become a reality.

I had faced a sudden insight into the actuality of death before. I was a shy and timid child, not much given to adventure, but this gradually changed after I left school, especially when I began travelling during university holidays. So, in my early twenties, I allowed myself to be persuaded by a friend to go parachute jumping. This involved a full day of training on the ground before making our first jump in the evening.

We went up to 2,500 feet in a small plane in batches of three, accompanied by the jump-master. As the Cessna circled the drop zone, we rehearsed the drill. "Put your right foot down through the open door onto the step. Lean out and grasp the wing strut with your right hand. Pull yourself out. Grasp the strut with your other hand as well, and change feet. When your left foot is securely on the step, your right foot will be trailing in the wind. With both hands on the wing struts, turn to look at the jump-master. When he gives the signal, let go, pushing yourself backwards. In the air, assume the spread-eagle position, counting slowly to four. By this time, your parachute will have opened."

It sounded straightforward, but the first person in my group panicked after getting out of the plane. He hung on tightly when the jump-master told him to push away. As the plane continued over the drop zone, the window of opportunity narrowed. He would soon be in danger of falling near power lines or traffic. The tension rose as the jump-master grew increasingly angry and impatient, leaning out to try and force the frightened jumper into releasing his grip. Eventually, he did let go. Suddenly, it was my turn.

I was determined not to make the jump-master angry and to follow the drill, but I had a shock when I tried to pull myself out of the plane. It had been easy at ground level during practice, but the air was now rushing past at almost a hundred miles an hour. It took a great deal of both physical and mental effort to get myself in position. When the jump-master told me to go, instead of pushing off I simply let go.

Despite knowing that my parachute would open automatically, and that if it didn't, I had a reserve chute to deploy; when I was looking down, standing on that small aircraft step, feeling the rushing wind, it was like facing death in the face. All my instincts, like those of the previous jumper, were to hang on and try getting back into the plane. I was momentarily terrified. My mind was so completely full of naked fear that, when given the signal, I went completely blank. I had no energy or willpower left, either to hang on or to push myself off. I just fell.

Fortunately, of course, the chute did open three and a half seconds later, and I had the joyful experience for a minute and a half of floating gently back to earth. My mind was suddenly clear again as I drank in the lovely scene. It was a beautiful summer's evening, and the countryside laid out tidily below me, formed an impressive picture of rural splendour. The next day, I went up again.

This brief encounter with the real possibility of my own death, accompanied briefly by extreme, mind-numbing fear, followed by survival and tranquillity, left me changed. This was a miniature death-and-rebirth kind of experience, and I was a much less fearful person afterwards. A new kind of faith in my continued existence gave a boost to my baseline level of courage. It was a small but significant breakthrough. I knew that I had not actually faced death, and did not think I would have to for many years, but my grandfather's last words continued hauntingly to affect me. I was going to be revisiting fear. Would it be followed again by relief?

Grandad had faced his death with joyful equanimity. By the time I met the clairvoyant Mrs Woodcock, I had also experienced the final illness, transformation and death of Mrs Cruikshank. I was heartened by seeing her life come to a kind of victorious conclusion. I had seen other patients die much less well prepared. Something else was also about to happen to bring the negative and painful aspects of death into my mental reality.

Less than a year after my grandfather died, a few months after I met Mrs Woodcock, a friend, someone I loved very dearly, also developed cancer. She was in her thirties. The early signs were such that her doctors thought it safe simply to watch the breast lump, but two years later it suddenly grew and needed surgical removal. By the time of the operation, the medical team had discovered the cancer to have spread widely into my friend's bones. She would have chemotherapy, but her chances of long-term survival were slim. I heard the news by telephone. My friend was in tears as she told me how I had been right, and she wished she had listened to my advice to have the original lump removed and examined.

I remember crying myself when I put the phone down. I felt sorrow, but bitterness too because my recommendations had not been heeded. The world at that time seemed very dark. I decided to go for a long walk. It was a Saturday. I drove to a popular beauty spot a few miles away, feeling very negative. Amazingly, in the car park, I met a work colleague and his wife, and with them was their new daughter, less than two weeks old. Her name was Joy. So, even here in my dark moment, a magical ray of sunlight had managed to penetrate. This chance or perhaps cosmically inspired meeting took the edge off my gloom. There was a future to hope in after all.

I could not visit my dying friend. Circumstances had separated us, and she was living in another city, hundreds of miles away. It was as if I was being left by God and the Universe to ponder the mysteries of life and especially of death, to try and make new sense of them.

Grandad's Koan

My grandfather's final comment was like a Zen koan. It was a riddle with no obvious solution that I felt committed to solve, but I was not properly equipped until several months later when I met the Buddhist monk and began learning how to meditate.

In the meantime, I tried to ask myself if I would do anything differently if I were indeed to die at the end of four years. This was helpful. Anyone can die at any time. Remember how close Doug had got to sudden death, pulled into the torrent at Graveyard Rapids on the Spanish River. Accidents happen. People get ill. Why should I be exempt? Four more guaranteed years for my friend with spreading cancer would be a decided bonus. What was it all about? I felt I needed to know.

It was a time for re-examining my values, for re-evaluating what gave meaning and a sense of purpose to my life. I decided that a large part of it was my work, training to become a psychiatrist. It seemed particularly important that my life be useful to others in some way, and this path seemed to have been chosen for me. It felt perfectly right, as if I was simply born to follow it. This was comforting, so I threw myself with renewed vigour into my study and work.

Reflection

Think again about what part fear, anger and sadness play in your life. Can you imagine fear ever being liberating? Does sorrow sometimes bring comfort?

18. Finding Compassion

Much of my training took place in a large mental hospital, before such institutions became unfashionable and started to close. My duties included visiting what we referred to then as the back wards. These were the places where people with severe and disabling forms of long-term mental illness were housed and treated. It was supposed to be routine work, responding to nurses' requests to write up medication charts, attend to minor physical ailments among the patients, and so on; but I became interested in these nearly-forgotten cases, whose illnesses had not responded satisfactorily to treatment. I often found their circumstances distressing.

One man in his early forties, I remember, was distressed and tearful on a daily basis. He seemed perpetually tormented by grief and absorbed by self-pity, but it was hard to understand why. "Help me! Help me!" He cried out over and over. His thought patterns were very disturbed and, despite large doses of medication, he was incoherent and inconsolable most of the time. I asked my teachers about this man, Marcus, thinking that there must surely be something else we could try; but I was only told not to worry about him. Everything that could be done for him had been and was being done. I was advised to concentrate my time and energies elsewhere, where they might be more productive. I should leave Marcus to the care of the mental health nurses who were used to him and his ways.

A cup of tea with Marcus

We did have excellent psychiatric nurses, both disciplined and caring. I respected them and their judgement, but I still wanted to try and do more for Marcus. I went to see him daily for a time, hoping to break through to him somehow; but only once did there seem to be any sensible communication between us.

I had been visiting him regularly for about three weeks. I was standing with him in the patch of garden behind the ward building, beginning sadly to realise that my teachers might be right and that I was wasting my time. At that moment, I am sure that I was even more distressed than Marcus. During a lull in my latest attempt to begin a dialogue with him, when I could think of nothing further to say, he had turned away from me and wandered off a few paces. I must have just stood there looking miserable, because he soon returned, came up behind me and clapped me on the shoulder as if I were an old friend.

"Come on,' he said in my ear. "Let's go and have a cup of tea."

Then, tugging at my arm, Marcus led me back inside. This was astonishing. He had never shown any sign of mutuality with others before. It was a humbling moment, because it felt like a complete reversal of our normal roles. Marcus was taking care of me. By the time we reached the tea-room, rejoining the nurses and other patients, he was as incoherent in his speech as usual. Having completed his rescue of me, he soon wandered away again, lost once more in a world of his own.

This was the only time I ever heard Marcus say anything significantly intelligible, and he seems to have done so as a way of setting me free from my pain. I read into it that he appreciated my concern, but that he wanted to reassure me that I need not worry excessively about him. At some profound level, he seemed to understand that the universe was perfect. Even in his misery, he seemed able to recognize that he was somehow all right. I may be exaggerating this, but I found these ideas comforting now that I had to face the facts about my inability to assist him. Wanting him to get better did not help. It only led me to suffer.

At about the same time, I had responsibility for another patient. Don was younger than Marcus, about nineteen, and was suffering from a cruel mixture of schizophrenia and depression. Don frequently heard derogatory voices and believed himself to be persecuted. Sometimes the voices told him he was so unworthy that he should die, and Don had attempted suicide several times. His wrists bore some of the scars, and he had taken several medication overdoses.

Some of the time, though, unlike Marcus, Don's mood and mental state improved. During these positive fluctuations, he appeared very likeable. He was particularly interested in motorbikes, and would read motorcycle magazines regularly. He was tall and physically healthy, popular with both the nurses and the other patients. Because his condition went up and down, we needed to monitor him closely and adjust his medications accordingly. My job was to interview him daily and report to my consultant for advice about treatment for Don.

Engaging with Don's family

Living alone in a rented house at that time, I had hired a cleaner,

Pauline, for a few hours each week. I used to visit Pauline and her husband after work to pay her. One day, to my surprise, she asked about Don. It is not usual to discuss patients away from work, so I asked why she wanted to know about him and how she knew I was involved with his care at the hospital. She told me that she was his sister.

This brought something home to me that I had often been guilty of neglecting when working with patients. They were family members with parents, siblings and perhaps children who loved and cared about them. These people naturally wanted information and to be involved in their relative's care.

A few days later Pauline brought her mother and sister to my office at the hospital for a discussion. I had to say that we were doing our best for Don, but that his illness was responding only partially and intermittently to our treatment. I was worried that he might end up in a back ward like Marcus, but did not say so. I told them honestly that I did not know how things would go.

A few weeks later, I was able to present Don's case to Professor John Strauss, a visiting American expert on schizophrenia. He heard my case history and, very sympathetically and at great length, interviewed Don himself. In the end, the kind professor had to agree that we were doing all that was possible. This, of course, was both frustrating and reassuring at the same time. I remember speaking to Pauline and her mother about it at another meeting we held.

There is no satisfactory ending to this tale, because Don suffered a reaction to all the attention he was getting. He seemed to be expecting a miraculous cure and, when he did not improve, he relapsed into a dark depression, taking to his bed for several days. When he emerged, he refused to let me interview him again, so his case was re-allocated to one of my colleagues. Soon afterwards, I went to work in another part of town, at the Children's Hospital for six months as a normal part of my training rotation. During this time, Pauline found full-time work and stopped cleaning my house, so I do not know the outcome. I can only hope and pray that Don's life somehow improved.

The difficulties I was having in my work with people like Marcus and Don did have one positive effect at the time. The Buddhist monk who taught us meditation at the two-day Jung workshop stayed in the city for a week before returning to Tara House, a Tibetan Buddhist centre in Melbourne where he was based, and I had the opportunity of several long conversations with him. I do not recall the Tibetan name he had been given by the Dalai Lama when he became a monk, but he told me to call him by his original name, Scott.

Learning about suffering

I described to Scott the cases of Marcus and Don, and my personal distress at not being able to assist them. He listened attentively, and then asked where the suffering was. I repeated that both Marcus and Don were suffering immensely. He looked at me kindly, and repeated, "But, Larry, where is the suffering you are telling me about?"

It took a moment for me to realize that he meant I was suffering.

"It's here", I said, pointing to my heart.

"That's right", Scott told me. "And why are you suffering?"

I could not immediately think of an answer.

"Why are you suffering?" Scott insisted.

I shook my head. He answered for me.

"You are suffering,' he said, "Because you care".

Scott told me that the cause of my suffering was a good cause – it was compassion.

'It hurts to care,' he said, 'And there is no way around that. "Com-passion" comes from Latin. It means "to suffer with". Your job is to protect yourself and learn how to grow.'

He went on to explain that suffering usually means pain, either emotional, physical or both; but another meaning of the word is simply 'to experience', without feeling any pain. You can suffer heat or cold, for example, in a detached way or with the kind of fortitude that takes the distress out of it.

Finally Scott said that to suffer can also mean 'to allow'. In a well-known bible story, Jesus says, "Suffer the little children to come unto me", meaning let them come, or even encourage them to come. Scott thought that this meaning held the key to suffering.

'If you allow it, it will hurt less than if you resist it. Feeling bad is not the problem. *Feeling bad about feeling bad*: that is the problem. If you feel bad about feeling bad, you always try and resist. If you resist emotional pain, you strengthen it. If you suppress it, it will find a way to revisit you more forcefully until you have to take notice.'

This certainly seemed to be true in my case at that time. I was discussing my emotional distress over Marcus and Don with Scott because I was resisting it. I wanted it to stop; yet it seemed only to grow. His pointing out that it had a good, natural and unstoppable cause – compassion – helped me to accept it and stop resisting it. It was a kind of conversion, changing and vastly improving my attitude to my work thereafter.

Scott's words and interpretation of the situation allowed me to stop feeling bad about my distress at not being able to help Marcus and Don. It was not my fault that they were ill, and that their illnesses were difficult to treat. I could feel good about my pain, because it came from a worthy source: my capacity to care for the unfortunate. I did not have to feel ashamed or guilty any longer – I could start feeling good about feeling bad.

Wisdom and compassion

This was Scott's gift to me. He pointed out that wisdom without compassion is not true wisdom, and that compassion without wisdom leads only to exhaustion and further distress. It can be tough, recognising and accepting your limits, but now I could see how important it was to do so with candour and honesty.

I understood that I had needed to grow in wisdom so that I could suffer, in the sense of experience, what was formerly painful without the same degree of pain. I would now suffer more in the second sense of the word, with a degree of equanimity. This in turn would permit me to grow further, reaching a point of actually welcoming engagement with the distress of others, fostering my own compassionate reaction, however momentarily painful.

I realized that, even if you can do nothing else, sharing someone's pain with them often has a calming and healing effect upon them. To be able to do so with equanimity is a kind of spiritual skill to acquire and develop, because it is decidedly therapeutic. It is slightly regrettable only that I had to go outside my profession to learn this in such a meaningful way.

Scott recommended that I engage thoroughly with patients like Marcus and Don, taking them to heart as teachers. They were teaching me about myself, about my true values, and about how much I care for others as fellow human beings, even when they are apparently strangers.

"People who cause you pain are most valuable," Scott said. "They show you where you are holding on, where your passion, your attachments and aversions are strongest. You need to become aware of these before you can go to work and release yourself from them. This is why the historical Buddha, like Christ, taught that we should love our enemies. It is not so much for their benefit as for our own."

This all seemed to make sense. It made me change my attitude towards severe and enduring forms of mental illness too. I had seen them as blights, to be eradicated as soon as possible. Now I thought of them differently, more positively. These conditions can teach us what nothing else can about valuing the faculties of a healthy mind, which so many take for granted until they begin to disappear, either abruptly or gradually. It occurred to me that losing your mind, through a condition like unresponsive schizophrenia or Alzheimer's disease, would be comparable to losing your life. Facing mental illness is something like facing death, in that it can teach you about what really matters.

Recognizing this helped me again with my struggle over my grandfather's final words. I had been taking my own intelligence, emotional life, capacity for sense perceptions, speech and action for granted, as well as any higher powers of creativity and intuition I had discovered within myself. These experiences, and the ability to appreciate both the activity of my mind and its stillness, have helped me to value mental abilities as much as bodily function while I continue to breathe. Conscious awareness often seems more important than bodily health. We are attached to life, and usually seek to prolong it. Are there values that go beyond that?

Reflection

Have you noticed that caring about people in distress makes you suffer too?

Do you generally resist painful emotions? Do you ever feel bad about feeling bad?

---

19. Solving the Riddle

Three years after he made it, I was still intensely preoccupied by my grandfather's apparently prophetic final remark – 'See you in four years.' One night, I had a remarkable dream.

I was walking along, close to the right side of a brightly lit tunnel, like a subway or underground tunnel. The walls were coated with shining white tiling and, from somewhere ahead of me, a brilliant glow was bathing the whole scene in light. At first, the tunnel was empty, and I was feeling calm. Quite soon, though, I experienced a rush of wind, and immediately knew that I was being pursued by something or someone malevolent. My mood changed to one of anxiety and apprehension.

At this point, I half-turned my head to the left and saw three black-cloaked figures carrying automatic weapons. They were in a hurry. I knew somehow that they were not after me, but that they would have no patience with anyone likely to obstruct them. I felt afraid, and at that moment the three men opened fire, spraying the tunnel indiscriminately. The noise was deafening and deadly bullets started to ricochet around. Even though they were not aimed directly at me, I felt sure I would be hit. My sense of foreboding and terror intensified as I hunched my shoulders, lowered my head and pressed myself against the wall.

My attempt to make myself invisible failed because, in the next moment, I was hit. A high-powered bullet entered my head, smashing my skull and pulverising my brain. I slumped against the tunnel wall, as my blood coated the tiling; but somehow I was still conscious. Despite unsurvivably fatal wounds, I continued to live.

I soon woke up, still sweating. The dream, which had seemed so real, represented another amazing death and rebirth experience, as had the parachute jump. The anxiety passed and I was left feeling elated. This is a measure of how possessed I had become with the possibility that I had less than a year to live. In any case, I knew that death was inevitable. The idea of survival beyond it as suggested by the dream was very appealing. I had been thinking of physical death as very final, an endpoint. This dream, however strange, made me feel much less concerned.

The memory that my grandfather had been smiling took on greater significance. I could see him again in my mind's eye. It was as if he was encouraging me to solve the riddle his words had set, because I would reap a valuable prize.

On the Road

My anxious feelings of anticipation were set aside temporarily as a result of this dream of reprieve. Soon afterward, I was driving my open-top car along a South Australian highway, heading east with the ocean and the setting sun to the rear. I remember singing along to cheerful songs on my tape-deck, happily amazed at the quality of the light, the fabulous interplay of pinks, reds and yellows on the clouds above and the tranquillity of the rural scenery before me. It was a gorgeous summer evening, and I was in a carefree and utterly joyful mood. The music stopped as a tape finished. I drove on in silence for a few minutes. The thought then suddenly occurred to me that, whenever death came, whether soon or at a great age, I would have to let go of all this. I would lose everything of what, a moment earlier, had seemed like an earthly paradise. Tears quickly welled up in my eyes. I could no longer see and had to pull the car over.

I was so aware that everything that I had ever enjoyed would be gone, taken away by that tyrant, death. Out of the blue, my mind had been totally filled with sadness. I was grieving for myself. It was intense, but after crying quite hard for several minutes, I started to feel cleansed and much better.

It was as if, through the intuition of my wisdom mind, I was being reorientated to the present moment. This too equates with the contemplative mentality of the Sabbath, with the here and now directly and mysteriously linked to eternity. We have what we have in the present moment only. This was something I was beginning to realize clearly for the first time. We cannot enjoy anything forever. Nevertheless, the prospect of losing things need not detract from the enjoyment we experience while we are having them. This was another reversal for me, another conversion moment, a kind of epiphany. Instead of trying to secure and hold onto pleasurable experiences, I began more calmly letting them go, at the same time enjoying them all the more fully when present.

I was discovering that this relaxed attitude completely defuses the threat associated with loss. Without the need to hold on so tightly to what seems important, anxiety and the threat of sorrow are replaced naturally by inner peace, spontaneity and joy. To pre-empt and disarm threats and losses reduces similarly the risk of painful emotions and enhances their pain-free complementary forms. It permits a comforting and essentially joyful degree of emotional detachment. This was to take me some time to adjust and get used to, nevertheless this on-the-road experience was another helpful lesson as I approached the big crossroads of mortality.

My grandfather's final communication was changing me, and the pace of change was speeding up. At about the same time, I had another curious but positive dream. This was about my friend whose cancer was now invading her bones. I knew enough as a doctor to predict – accurately as it transpired – that her life would be extended by radiotherapy and chemotherapy, but that her condition would eventually prove fatal. She was to die about three years after her operation.

When she appeared in my dream, though, it seemed again to discount the idea of death as something final. It seemed to be about love between two people transcending earthly time; that as long as one of the pair was alive, so would the love that they had discovered or generated between them be alive. It would remain a powerful influence on the survivor as a source of comfort and wisdom.

My friend was still living, and I did see her again before she died, so this was not a communication from beyond the grave. It was, I think now, my wisdom mind telling me wholemindedly again something about the timeless nature and benevolent powers of love. The two dreams and that evening drive through the glorious Australian countryside primed and prepared me for facing my own death, but I still had to go through the fear.

It does not surprise me that initiation rites within aboriginal tribal cultures throughout the world, for the men at least, involve finding courage through enduring something potentially terrifying. This may either be some life-threatening experience, or the artificial arousing of fear through the use of hallucinogenic drugs like mescaline and peyote. As I discovered when I learned to parachute, extreme fear has a liberating effect on the mind after survival. It is a kind of induced catharsis of fear.

Face to face with death

My own moment of initiation arrived early one morning, well into the fourth of the four years. This was when wide awake, I met my death face to face and survived. It was symbolic, but felt real.

I was living in an Australian colonial-style bungalow with a verandah and a corrugated iron roof. I was woken in the night by a thunderstorm. The noise of the rain beating on the roof was intense. I had spent the previous day preoccupied with thoughts of death, strangely resigned to my fate, whatever it might prove to be. You might think I was foolish to pay so much attention, and give so much credence, to the idea that my grandfather had accurately foretold my death, and I thought so too. It was stupid. However, I simply could not ignore his words and get on with life. The riddle had to be solved and the situation resolved. My best guess was that I would survive the four years, and that the significance of the words would stay a mystery; but this was not what occurred. There was to be a definitive outcome.

I fell asleep again that night with the rainfall still pounding down. In the morning, however, the storm had passed. The clouds had dispersed and the sky was completely blue. As I looked through the curtains, I could see the leaves on the trees and bushes glistening brightly, dripping with diamond-clear droplets of water. In such a dry place as Adelaide, this was really a blessing. My mood was as bright as the sunlight. Then, when I opened my bedroom door, right in front of me was my death.

The symbol for my death that day took the form of a terrifying dragon. Here it was, boldly confronting me. It was in fact a large Australian lizard that must have entered my house seeking shelter from the rain. It would not normally seem so scary, but my mind was abruptly in turmoil, and I could only interpret this creature as the immediate herald of my death. I felt terror rising within me to the point almost of panic. At that instant, as I opened the bedroom door, all I wanted was to flee and hide; but something else within made me wait and stay my ground.

My heart had started racing. I heard rushing sounds in my ears and felt throbbing at my temples. I stared at the lizard who stared menacingly back. It was on the carpet less than two feet in front of me. 'It can't hurt you,' I tried to tell myself; but did not truly believe it.

Seconds passed, and I could not have felt more uncomfortable. Little by little, though, I realized that I was obviously still alive. There were choices that I could make. The moment of paralysis wearing off, I forced myself to get past the lizard, making it into another room where I closed the door and sat down, breathing heavily, quickly and uncontrollably shaken with both laughter and tears. A thorough release of emotional energy continued intermittently like this for some time. I sat for about thirty minutes before calming down, collecting my wits sufficiently to go and take a shower.

I had been laughing at my own stupidity, while crying too with relief. Although there had been nothing genuinely to fear, this was not how my mind had processed the information when confronted by that lizard.   Going to the shower, I no longer saw it in the passage, but it was back again when I returned to the bedroom. This time, however, I could see it clearly as just a harmless creature. It seemed smaller than at first, and more vulnerable than dangerous. This time, as I moved towards it, the lizard turned and hurried away. I was laughing again. My triumph over death was complete. I had faced it down. But I had not yet understood what my grandfather had meant by, "See you in four years".

Renewing bonds of love

This is how I interpret Grandad's message now. The key to under-standing is his love. My grandfather, George, loved me unconditionally. Until the day of my symbolic death facing that lizard, however, I had not recognized and appreciated the nature and extent of the spiritual bond between us. Now I can say that there were no barriers between us. On that day, I 'saw' my grand-father clearly for the first time. I saw and felt his love for me in full force, simultaneously experiencing my reciprocal love for him in return. It was as it must have been when I was an infant perched on his knee, in the scene described by Mrs Woodcock. That pre-conditioning moment had found its point of completion.

It was no longer, in my case, a selfish or possessive type of love that I felt for Grandad, as it had been when I was younger. It is natural for children to look upon their parents and grandparents as providers. My grandfather was poor, but at one time was a regular source of smiles and fun, sometimes too of sweets, treats and pocket-money. After his strokes and paralysis, and as I grew older, he naturally gave me less in the material sense. I stopped looking to him to provide. The roles were then gradually reversed. I came to see it as my duty to visit him regularly and provide what I could for him, both in terms of small gifts and by trying to boost his morale during my visits. I always felt rather sad and helpless going to see him. I usually felt that I should make the pilgrimage more often, but was sometimes selfish about it. He was never much of a conversationalist, but he did manage to convey his appreciation, so until I went overseas I had been going every few weeks to his house.

Strangely, it was only now, after this moment of emotional release, that I could accept fully that he was gone. Paradoxically, in my mind's eye, he had become more alive than ever. I no longer thought of him as disabled, disadvantaged or distressed by his paralysis. I remembered, and remember him still, only smiling, relaxed and content. Whenever I think of him, as I also think of the friend who died of her cancer more than twenty years ago, I experience and am conscious only of powerful and comforting warmth, approval and love. It is an extraordinary blessing, the concomitant of which has been the recognition that this love expresses the true nature of the bond between all human beings.

In the spiritual dimension, everyone is connected to everyone else. What one person thinks, says and does influences the whole. Individual thoughts, words and actions affect and influence the sacred unity of the universe. They leave a trace, and so alter conditions for everyone else. This is the reality. This is the call to individual responsibility. This is the basis for selfless, *spiritual* values to be regarded as true and superior to the false, selfish, materialistic values with which they often appear to be in competition.

The word for 'evil' in some Middle Eastern languages can also be translated as 'unripe'. This is a hopeful idea. It implies immaturity, and therefore the possibility of further growth. Evil can, under the right growing conditions, be transformed into good. The necessary healing environment, the growth medium, will depend upon wisdom, compassion and love. Spiritual growth and development, as a rule, occur in recognizable stages. We all begin as immature beings: physically, psychologically, socially and spiritually. In the next chapters, we are going to look at stages of spiritual growth.

Reflection

Have you had any big dreams that seem to have been particularly significant? Have you had any brushes with death, either real or symbolic?

If the answer to either question is 'yes', spend some time reflecting on the dream or the occasion.

---

20. Faith, Hope and Psychiatry

Facing down that symbolic dragon of death, the Australian lizard, I finally resolved my grandfather's last riddle by awakening to the power of selfless love. I realized it is the self-centred and acquisitive ego that dies, not the person; and that when the ego dies, it reveals something greater. Ego-death allows the true self, timelessly in tune with the totality of a sacred universe, to emerge. It releases a huge expansion of a person's horizons, and heralds the arrival of faith.

The difference between faith and belief

Experiencing faith is different from holding a belief. Faith includes all arguments and cannot be challenged successfully. The notion of belief, however, implies the simultaneous possibility of doubt. From the perspective of faith, then, beliefs are nothing less than strong forms of attachment to an idea or set of ideas about something. A belief is like a strongly held opinion, which we have the power to choose – often according to our own personal, occasionally selfish agendas

The choice may be conditioned by upbringing and circumstances. It may be unconscious, and so it may not feel that we have actually made choices. Nevertheless, as we advance through adulthood, such centrally guiding principles in our lives are naturally called into question. We need to express and examine them, if we are to mature.

Holding a belief, like holding any attachment, renders you

vulnerable to the threat of loss when that belief is challenged –
either by events and experience, or by someone else with differing
beliefs. Hold a belief and you are immediately vulnerable to doubt,
bewilderment and all the painful emotions in the spectrum.

To defend yourself against the emotional discomfort and pain,
you may be inclined to hold all the more tightly to what you believe
and deny all challenges; but this only sets you up for further
conflict and more distress. Only when we realize that the source of
the conflict is internal, will we be able to start putting things right
and find our way again towards peace and contentment.

Faith includes everything

Faith in a totality that includes all possibilities, on the other hand,
cannot give rise to conflict. It is faith in a reality where opposites
cancel out and negate each other, where all contradictions are
resolved over time. To understand this depends on wisdom, on
discovering a kind of Taoist perspective, recognizing the eternal
dynamic interplay between yin and yang. Conflict avoidance
and conflict resolution can come about only by mature 'both/and'
thinking.

It may take a long time for newly sown seeds of faith to grow
sufficiently strong and extensive for peace to reign, even in one
person's heart. To try and answer the question, "what do you have
faith in?" you can only answer, "everything". You accept as whole
and perfect the mysterious and dynamic entirety. If you have been
trained in 'either/or' thinking, you may find that difficult; but when
you take the humble road, begin to grasp the truth behind it, and
feel a stirring at least of the inkling of faith, then you will find a

powerful source of both guidance and courage. Look within. Meditation and other spiritual practices all assist in this discovery process.

After my prophesied encounter with death; this spiritual conversion, breakthrough, awakening or whatever it was; I spent three days in a mild state of bliss and euphoria. I was seeing and understanding things differently. It was like being able to appreciate the same situation from every point on the compass, from everyone's point of view, at the same time.

A new perspective at work

I was working at the Adelaide Children's Hospital. People there noticed a difference in me and remarked upon it, but I could not explain what had happened, and did not try. In particular, with my own personal and self-seeking life agenda on hold, I had a much improved intuitive awareness of other people, including the parents and children with whom I was working. Accordingly, one or two cases ended with very satisfying results. Because I could see what was going on so clearly, I knew what to say that would be helpful. More importantly, I knew when to remain silent. I was able to pay especially close attention to what was not being said, but was being articulated through non-verbal communication – looks and gestures in particular – and through the emotional tone in the room. I could read it all like a book.

Sometimes in a session, the atmosphere grew very tense. In one family, Kevin, a young boy, had been getting recurrent abdominal pain with no apparent underlying physical abnormality to explain it. I interviewed him alone and then with his parents and younger brother. Two older brothers of working age were unable to attend. I suggested that there could be tension in the family to which Kevin was reacting. What did they think it might be? After a brief denial from both parents, there was a long silence. The two young boys eventually grew fidgety, so I let them return to the waiting area where there were toys. Kevin's parents agreed to stay, but remained silent. They insisted that they were getting along well with each other, neither were there any problems with their older sons, the older of whom worked with his father.

Eventually, more than an hour from the start of the session, I noticed that *I* was feeling the tension in *my* abdomen. It was almost painful. I assumed that I was reacting in the same way as Kevin, and this made me confident that I was still on the right track. Finally, the mother frowned and reluctantly said she had something to say that might have a bearing on the problem.

It transpired that Kevin's mother had dreamt, soon after the birth of her second son, that he would die. When she awoke, she 'knew' that this would happen if she told anyone. She could only protect him as long as she never spoke of her dream and its prophecy. It was her hidden anxiety, her dark secret. She had never confessed about it to anyone until this moment in that therapy room.

This son, Malcolm, aged about twenty, had survived. Nevertheless, his mother told us that he had always been different from her other sons. He was uncomfortable within this rural family of farmers. Finally arguing with his father during his teen years, he left the family home at the earliest opportunity. Now he was living in the city where he was studying the performing arts. His mother missed him a great deal. Her love for him was clearly very strong, as it was for her husband and other children. This division of her loyalty was a source of considerable pain, which she was still trying to deny and conceal.

I wondered aloud whether Malcolm's departure from the family had been a kind of symbolic death, and had felt like bereavement. The response was dramatic. Kevin's mother quietly started to cry.

After a while, her husband leaned across to comfort her, as we experienced a magical and immediate evaporation of the tension in the room. The pain in my stomach had also gone. I expected that Kevin's would disappear too now his mother's secret had been confessed and was in the open. I was also sure that there would be a change for the better in the family dynamics. The father, a silent but deep-thinking person, made it clear that he still loved his more difficult son. I knew that he would find a way to communicate his affection and respect, and work towards repairing the rift in the family. He supported his wife, and they both assured me that they could manage the situation henceforward. They were grateful, but firm in announcing that they did not need to see me again.

A few weeks earlier, I would not have had the patience or the courage to sit in silence, sharing Kevin's family's pain, until an explanation – and his mother's cathartic release of tears – was forthcoming. I had become, and have remained, a much more intuitive psychiatrist. I have often said things knowing them to be right, but without knowing exactly why. This is a problem only when trying to explain my decisions to other psychiatrists. I have found it best to let the results speak for themselves.

During my career, there have been many improvements in the conditions under which we practice psychiatry. I returned to

England in the early 1980s. The closure of the large psychiatric hospitals took place towards the end of that decade, and this was difficult, partly because replacement services were under-planned and under-resourced. Nevertheless, many younger people, who might once have been confined for long periods, have benefited from the newer policies and now live relatively comfortable and fruitful lives in the community.

This is partly because we have better treatments. In particular, we have clozapine – a form of medication used in cases of schizophrenia. It works in about two-thirds of the more severe cases, which have not responded to other drugs. I would have liked to try it on both Marcus and Don, for example, but it was not available when I was working in Australia. Of the two-thirds of patients that clozapine benefits, there is at least some improvement in about half, and a dramatic level of re-integration and recovery in the remainder. As schizophrenia is very common, affecting about one in a hundred people worldwide, this is extremely important and heart-warming. About half of my current patients are taking this medication. Here is the story of one of them, who has done remarkably well.

Bridget's Story

I first encountered Bridget after I became a consultant in 1988. She was then in her mid-thirties, suffering from schizophrenia. Like many other cases, this illness began when she was in her teens, and prevented her from completing her schooling. Her concentration was badly affected and she was unable to work. As a result, she could not earn money and needed state benefit payments. This was bad enough, but there were also persistently unpleasant and baffling experiences. For hours at a time every day, Bridget heard loud voices. These were just like real voices, although no one else could hear them. They were many and unkind, male and female voices calling her foul names, making derogatory comments to each other about her, and often telling her insistently that she should kill herself as she was worthless and would be better off dead. Imagine living with that!

Bridget was not my patient when I first encountered her. She was, however, living in a group-home near my office. On warm days, when I opened the first floor window, I frequently heard Bridget talking back to her voices. She often shouted, swearing loudly and repeatedly at them, insisting that they leave her alone. Her profanities could be heard the length and breadth of this leafy residential street. It was distracting whenever I was trying to concentrate or interview someone. It would not have been right to keep Bridget indoors. She had already spent several years locked away in a large mental hospital, and her treatment was relatively ineffective.

Fortunately clozapine, which became available in the UK in the early 1990s, worked for Bridget. Although it is not clear why people with schizophrenia hear voices, some brain mechanism must be involved because, with the new treatment, Bridget's voices gradually faded and eventually simply stopped. She was gradually able to start her life again. She still became tired easily and her powers of concentration, although improved, were still impaired, but as her voices evaporated so did her anti-social behaviour. There was no more irate and disruptive shouting up and down the street, in local shops and cafés.

Bridget had always been angry with her voices, and this anger had spilled over into most aspects and relationships of her life like a kind of poison. She mistrusted people, even members of her own family, and there had been a near-complete breakdown in communication between them. Sadly, her father had died before she became well again. Her mother was elderly, had diabetes, and with it both heart trouble and poor eyesight. One of Bridget's two sisters had gone to live overseas.

Bridget's new tasks on recovery included repairing the damage within the family. I have no way of proving it, but it seems to me after almost thirty years in psychiatry that a very high percentage of people with severe and enduring mental illnesses like schizophrenia have fine personalities underneath their symptoms. They are often super-sensitive, for example, to how others around them are feeling. I do not know if this level of sensitivity is part of the problem, increasing the person's vulnerability to the disorder they develop, or whether it is the illness and associated experiences that shape them, making them kinder and more tolerant than they would otherwise have been. Perhaps both are at work. Either way, I count it a blessing and a privilege to encounter and work with such people every day. Bridget was no exception, and she was able to get close to her mother and sisters again fairly quickly when, without the voices, her anger subsided completely, revealing kind and generous aspects of her true personality. Her grateful mother said it was a gift, like having her real daughter back again after a painful absence of so many years.

Another of Bridget's main tasks during this period of rehabilitation was to grieve the series of losses she had experienced: the loss not only of family relationships, now being restored, but also of her youth, her earlier hopes and ambitions, her ability to complete her education, to work and earn money, to find a partner and settle down, to raise her own family. These aspects, the direct consequences of her illness, were not so easily recovered or replaced, but Bridget understood and accepted this. She always told me that there were so many people much worse off than she felt herself to be.

Bridget's schizophrenia had robbed her of much of what we normally think of as essential for joy and satisfaction in life. She had to let go of these goals before she could move on... and was able to do so. I think of Bridget, and many like her, not only as a survivor but as a kind of hero; an example of someone who, through adversity, has discovered a healthy set of values and way of coping with life.

For administrative reasons to do with where she was living, Bridget came under my care six or seven years after she started taking the successful medication. By this time, she was not only friends again with her mother, who had once disowned her entirely, but was planning to move in to help look after her. She had also renewed her love for her sisters. With her mother and locally based sister, she made a short and successful visit to America, and there discovered the joys of being an aunt to very young nephews and nieces, the children of her other sister. On her return, I could detect only delight, and no trace of envy for what might have been if she had never been unwell in the first place. Bridget was facing reality.

This was the woman I came to know after she first attended my clinic a few years ago. Bridget needs a regular blood test to check that the clozapine is not harming her, and she returns to my clinic once or twice a year for a general mental health check-up. I always look forward to her visits because I remember how disturbed and distressed she once was, and so remind myself that however bleak a situation may seem, there is always hope for improvement. I also look forward to seeing her because of her gratitude and her intensely joyful demeanour. Bridget has so little in comparison with others – her contemporaries from her schooldays before the illness struck, for example – yet she always seems perfectly content.

When I ask her about this positive outlook, she readily explains by recounting the riches that sustain her: her loving family, her rich friendships and one more particular thing – her voluntary work. Two or three times a week, Bridget goes to help in the kitchens and serve meals at a day-care centre for the infirm elderly. She enjoys the work and also the social atmosphere, the conversation. She feels useful, needed and valued there. It is a place where she feels she truly belongs.

One of the most important aspects of Bridget's life is that she makes a regular contribution. By helping in even a small way to improve the lives of others, she feels rightly that she is giving something back. This is something that gives her life meaning and affords her a genuine and valued sense of purpose. It delights her also, not of course that her mother is almost blind, but that she is there to be her mother's eyes and help her, and to protect her from loneliness in her widowhood.

It is remarkable that someone who spent several years hidden away in hospital, as Bridget did, someone whose existence was more or less completely discounted at one time, could have something to teach the rest of us about values and how to enjoy a meaningful life; but this is how it is. For Bridget the recipe for happiness is simple: cultivate loving and trusting friendships; take each day as it comes; be grateful for what you have and share it, however little; think, speak and act when you can with kindness and compassion; be honest, especially with yourself; and accept limitations – your own and those of others.

Bridget herself might not say that she was humble, but humility is what she has learned and exemplifies. I would say for our benefit.

Reflections

Does the notion of belief imply the existence of doubt?

Which, if any, of your beliefs do you consider unshakeable?

Which, being honest, are more like strongly held opinions?

Can you think of arguments, and any evidence, against them?

What do you think of Bridget's recipe for happiness? Might it work for you, too?

21. A Cautionary Tale

Keith came to me for help when he was thirty-five. He had been experiencing occasional episodes of profound unhappiness for ten years. He had been able to think of obvious triggers in the past, but now he told me he was depressed about 'everything in general, yet nothing in particular'.

Keith had not seen a psychiatrist before attending my clinic. He had asked to do so now because the negative thoughts and painful feelings were more intense than previously. He had been feeling suicidal, carrying a length of hose in his car, ready to attach it to the exhaust system and asphyxiate himself if things got any worse. He was feeling hopeless, helpless and worthless, and had doubts about whether anyone else, me included, could help change things for the better. Before I could help, I needed to know more about him.

Keith's Story

Whereas Bridget's parents met, fell in love, married and had three daughters, were poor but supported each other and their children in a way that allowed them to grow up feeling secure and valued, the situation was different for Keith.

His father had been married and divorced by the time he met Keith's mother. Keith had two older half-brothers, whom he had never met because there was no contact between his father and his ex-wife or these boys. Keith had a younger full sister, and his father had another daughter as a result of an extra-marital relationship more recently, giving Keith a younger half-sister that he did not know about until she was ten, and whom he had also never met.

It is not surprising that Keith told me the family household when he was a child was 'not particularly happy' and his parents were 'not particularly close'. These, of course, were understatements. He said he remembered no open shows of affection within the family, and 'a lot of shouting'. They were materially comfortable, most of the time, because his father earned well; but he also had a penchant for casinos and gambling. This not only meant occasional episodes of financial insecurity and hardship, but also a father whose major interests lay elsewhere, outside his family.

As I got to know Keith, we came together to recognize the factors influencing his father from his unsatisfactory childhood. His father had brutalized him, and he came across as a sad, rather than a bad man.

Keith told me about himself that he lacked confidence at school, and failed to apply himself diligently as a result. He went from private to state education once when the company his father owned went bankrupt. With no real sense of purpose, Keith left school prematurely, aged seventeen, sure that he would fail his final exams if he had stayed on. He wanted to start earning money, to buy things and to become financially independent of his father. His first job, as a bank cashier, was, as he told me "dull but safe". Four years later, he became a trainee manager for a leisure company responsible for a chain of nightclubs. Keith surprised himself by eventually becoming a successful club manager, ascribing this to the fact that he did not like the effects of alcohol and always remained sober. Many others in the trade, he told me, drank excessively and under-performed as a result.

Like many people in late adolescence and young adulthood, Keith had spent several years experimenting with his lifestyle. He was not interested in drugs, but did go through a fairly promiscuous heterosexual phase. By his mid-twenties, though, thinking about acquiring more stability, he met Ann, and they began living together. Their child, Debbie, was born a year later and they decided to marry. Keith's self-confidence was still fragile, however. He worked long hours, protecting a self-esteem based heavily on employment success and a good level of income. It turns out that Ann was emotionally vulnerable too, and quickly felt neglected and undervalued by Keith. 'Ann decided I didn't love her,' he told me. 'One day, she just left with Debbie and went back to live with her parents.' The couple were eventually divorced. This simple description, of course, conceals a mountain of misery and recrimination.

This unhappiness led to the start of Keith's first major episode of depression. He got help from his local doctor, took medication for six months and had some counselling sessions, which helped. The treatment combination enabled him to carry on. He changed jobs within the same industry and moved from the Midlands to London, where the pay was better but the conditions worse. His hours of work increased significantly, especially at weekends, and his occasional contact meetings with Debbie became even rarer. As Keith threw himself back into work, he began feeling better temporarily. However, he became depressed again when another relationship failed, and he handled this too by moving away from the scene, further south. Unhappy with managing night-clubs, he started working for a multi-national alcoholic drinks manufacturer and distributor, and this was what he was doing when I saw him.

When he came to the first appointment, Keith had been selling alcohol for about five years. He had also started a new relationship, but felt unhappy with it. He found his work, driving around a large area of southern England, visiting pubs and night-clubs to persuade the managers to give preference to his company's brands, both fatiguing and unsatisfying. There was dishonesty involved. He was keen to admit that there is no significant difference in taste between several different brands of whisky or gin, for example, but he had always to maintain that his company's was superior. It increasingly felt to him like a lie.

Keith worried about losing his job, and blamed himself for a deteriorating performance. He had no energy for home life, and no appetite for socialising. His sexual drive and potency were reduced, so he worried that his girlfriend would leave him. Even a troubled relationship, he thought, was better than no relationship. It bothered him that he did not have the energy to change his way of life, or even really at times to care. He alternated between being anxious and apathetic. His pattern of sleep deteriorated, and so did his appetite.

This is a fairly standard description of an episode of depressive illness, and many of the symptoms would normally respond to adequate doses of medication. However, Keith had tried the prescriptions his doctor had again given him and, although the medication was partially helpful, there had been unpleasant side effects. His sexual performance became even worse, for example. More important for Keith was the persistent feeling that he was not in control of his own life. He did not want to rely on medication and asked my help to stop taking it. Given how suicidal he was feeling, I felt particularly uncomfortable with this request, but decided to take it seriously.

In general, there are two ways of dealing with emotional pain: to suppress it or to foster the healing and growth process by helping the pain to emerge. The ideal is the 'both/and' approach: to keep the worst of it under control, with medication if necessary, while encouraging gradual release. I have found that if medication is ineffective in some cases of depression, especially when the person resists taking it, there is no reason to persevere. It is best to trust the natural processes and the patient's own intuition.

Keith's treatment was generously being paid for by his employer, but there were restrictions on this. I could only see him once a month, and only for twelve months after the initial assessment. To start with, I asked Keith for his assurance that he would not attempt to kill himself before the next session; and he quickly agreed. Then, little by little, we went through his family background and life history again in more detail. This helped him get what had happened in better perspective, and he gradually learned to stop blaming himself for everything that seemed to go wrong. Keith was able to feel appropriate anger towards Ann for abandoning him without trying to understand him, but also to forgive her when he realized that she had her problems too. He was also able to feel appropriate sadness at losing Debbie.

During the year I saw Keith, Ann married someone else and negotiated through lawyers that her new husband be allowed to adopt Debbie, who was now about ten. Keith felt that giving up his legal rights as her natural father was the best thing he could do for her, but it was a genuine sacrifice and a most difficult decision. He still hopes that, after she turns eighteen, she will want to make contact with him again.

When Keith stopped blaming himself for past mistakes, and for everything that seemed to be going wrong in his present life, this was a major breakthrough. It helped that he had come to understand his father better, after talking to me and discussing matters with other family members. He had found the necessary courage, and the forgiveness in his heart, to make a special visit to see his father. It had not gone particularly well, but he felt better for making the effort. He also appreciated more fully what his mother had endured, and how much she was still there to love and support him. The unhappy relationship with his latest girlfriend came to a natural and mutually acceptable conclusion, and Keith started seeing someone else, about whom he felt much more positive. He also came off medication successfully during the year. His appetite, sleep pattern and sexual function all returned to normal. Before I said goodbye to him, Keith had started a part-time university course in archaeology. He was obviously a much happier and contented man, but there was still one thing on his mind.

'I feel I am in the wrong job,' he told me. ' I don't want to get to the end of my life knowing that I have only spent it selling alcohol to people.' He told me that a friend had left the company after deciding that working for it was socially irresponsible. Keith had defended the company at the time, pointing to their corporate policy on 'socially responsible drinking', but he too was becoming disillusioned.

Likening it to his own situation, Keith said that alcohol helps people suppress and ignore their true feelings. Ignoring distress only allows it to build up, making it more difficult to face and deal appropriately with later on. The risk of addiction was another undeniable feature. He had seen the alcohol-fuelled behaviour in pubs and especially night-clubs at first hand, and was being honest with himself in a way that he could not afford to when working there. 'There is something missing from their lives,' he told me. 'Getting drunk and drugged up, and all that goes with it, seems kind of soulless to me. You can't make good decisions when you're living like that.'

In our final session, confirmed in his subsequent letters, Keith mentioned that he had decided to retrain, either as a nurse or mental health nurse. In this, he has my full support. His days of depression may well be over. I hope so; but even if not, the episodic disorder is no bar to nurse training. His experiences will be an asset, in my view, rather than a weakness. Feeling genuinely useful in his working life will offset the risk of relapse.

Keith's story is instructive in a number of ways. The contrasting stories of Bridget and Keith, for example, demonstrate the important influence of families in our lives, whether mental illness is a factor or not. We began this book with the story of Kelly, who became pregnant and had the pregnancy terminated, later deciding in a more adult way with her boyfriend Brett to marry, commit themselves to each other and start a family. This seems to be the ideal – that children are planned and provided for, and in particular that they are wanted and loved. This was the case with Bridget, but only perhaps in the case of his mother with Keith. His father did not seem to want him, or any of his several children. As a result,

Keith had difficulties with confidence and self-esteem from his early days. Secondary to this, he had no sense of belonging in the social culture of his school, and no sense of direction or purpose as a student.

His response was to leave school to earn money and gain independence. He found a dull but safe job, growing a little in terms of assurance, enabling him to move into the more competitive and apparently exciting night-club management work; but even success at this, together with marriage and fatherhood, could not fill the emptiness left at the root of his being by his childhood. His vulnerable wife lost her fragile faith in him. He soon lost both Ann and his daughter, Debbie. His self-esteem had been shattered again. Every attempt he made to rebuild it, until he came into therapy, further damaged his self-belief, as he could not find any true meaning in life.

Spirituality: the perfect antidote

It is possible to describe this as clinical depression or a combination of anxiety and depression; of which we are presently seeing a near epidemic in our consumer culture; but it is also correct to think in terms of 'spiritual' dissatisfaction.

Spirituality is about many things, but perhaps especially relevant for a psychiatrist is the idea that it is at the heart of what gives life meaning, offering people both a genuine sense of purpose and a warm sense of belonging. It becomes a source of energy and motivation, the perfect antidote to depression.

Bridget's illness robbed her of education, employment opportunities, income-generating prospects, and the likelihood of getting married and raising a family. She was unlikely ever to become either rich or a celebrity, so no one would have been targeting her with their advertising. Since recovering from her illness with the help of clozapine and the renewed love of her family, she is among the happiest people I know. Her values are not acquisitive and materialistic; they seem both more genuine and robust. Bridget is content to have friends, a reason each day to get out of bed, a contribution to make to improve the lives of those around her, and through these a sense both of belonging and worth. This is all it takes to be happy.

Looking at the emotions involved, Bridget accepts her limitations, and has little cause for *self-doubt* or *bewilderment*. She has no substantial reason to feel *anxious*, *angry*, *guilty* or *ashamed*. She is no longer *sad*, having successfully grieved for what might have been. Avoiding the temptation to be competitive, she now enjoys sympathetically the happiness and successes of her sisters and friends. She does sometimes get irrational, illness-related moments of anxiety in specific situations, and she does need to continue to take medication, but without the usual markers of worldly success, her inner world is remarkably free of *wanting*, of both desire and aversion. This leaves her remarkably contented, joyful and calm.

Keith, on the other hand, tried to live according to the more obvious values of our culture, and found himself in conflict at the deepest level of his being. Many before him have also found that success and worldly pleasures are fragile and transitory, ultimately unsatisfying. Success, power, wealth, fame, sexual desire and the use of intoxicants are powerful distractions from life's essentially spiritual purpose: to be aware, to learn, to mature in terms of love, wisdom and compassion.

Worldly values and appetites like these are not in themselves necessarily destructive, but they are whenever they predominate over less selfish aims and spiritual values like honesty and trust, patience and perseverance.

Many people caught up in the pursuit of worldly success and celebrity, power and possessions, are responding to a deep-seated, and often unconscious rejection of insignificance and meaninglessness. We encountered an extreme and highly destructive example in chapter 4 in the case of the Nazis. Frequently in denial, such people are in reality demonstrating profound personal insecurity. Achieving their aims does nothing to change this. Get what you want, and nothing protects you from realizing that it is not secure or feeling that it is not enough. Get what you think is enough, and there is nothing to ward off a sense of satiety and protect you from the boredom and frustration of having more than you can use. Nothing can defend you either from the reality that death will one day arrive and take it all away.

In Tibetan Buddhist iconography, the deity-figure representing death, Mara, is called 'the one who knows'. Death knows everything about us, so the teaching goes, and we cannot escape its ultimate wisdom. The way forward is to accept, welcome and embrace the idea of death, as my grandfather's prophecy made me do, because only in acceptance can our egos find liberation from worldly values and the constant pressure to achieve material goals. Mental illnesses, I have found, often point in a similar direction.

The wisdom mind, 'the mind that knows', operates silently. It is frequently in conflict with the everyday mind of desire and attachment, with the self-centred ego of likes and dislikes. Because this conflict is the basis of anxiety, depression and all emotional pain, we need to understand it better. Intellectual understanding, however, is useless. We need to engage ourselves as emotional beings and as whole personalities, so this type of understanding involves a deeply personal quest. The conclusion is inescapable that we are each required to follow a spiritual journey of our own. Such journeys can be described as proceeding in stages. These are the stages of faith that we shall be looking at soon.

Reflections

What were the conditions of your childhood like? Were they mainly favourable, unfavourable or mixed?

How are you spending your life? What are your values? What are your goals?

What are your hopes? Have you hung on to some, or are they mostly invested in others (such as the next generation)?

22. Conditioning and Conformity

James Fowler's 1981 book *Stages of Faith*[33] is based on psychological research. It has something of an academic flavour and is not a particularly easy read. Nevertheless, the ideas proposed are intelligent; and they are useful because they seem to fit with reality and tell us a lot about ourselves. I am going to adapt, simplify and expand on this valuable material in this and succeeding chapters. Fowler himself describes borrowing and synthesizing ideas from three other writers and researchers on human psychological development: Jean Piaget, Lawrence Kohlberg and Erik Erikson[34].

Fowler and his colleagues put together a set of ideas about how people develop towards spiritual maturity in six stages throughout life. They then conducted research interviews with over 350 people to test their theories. We will concentrate here on stages three, four and five, because these are the stages most readers will find themselves identifying with and recognizing in family, friends and acquaintances; but it is necessary to begin by saying something about the earlier stages. I will also mention stage six. I have given new, less technical names to the stages, making them simpler.

---

[33] See 'Recommended Books and Websites'.

[34] Erikson's work is summarised in two small books: *Identity and the Life Cycle*, and *The Life Cycle Completed*. It is also the basis for Gail Sheehy's best-selling book, *Passages*. Details are listed under 'Recommended Books and Websites'.

Here is the list:

Egocentric
Conditioning
Conformist
Individual
Integration
Teaching & Healing

I want to begin by asking you to stop reading for a moment and try to recall your earliest memory. Simply shut your eyes, take a breath, let it go, and think back as far into your childhood as you can.

Some people are apparently able to recall being born, but this is rare. A good percentage of people, though, have memories dating from at least their first experiences of school. It is in infancy that we first become aware of ourselves as separate beings, as separate from others, and *in* but *apart from* our surroundings.

I have a vivid and somehow timeless memory of standing on top of a coal bunker beside the garage at home on a warm summer day. I was about three at the time, and recall surveying the back garden from this high vantage point with a sense of wonder. I seem to remember revelling in the power of motion. Did I pick up a stick and knock down flowers, then wave and hurl it about? The memory is vague. I was simply enjoying the capacity for movement and for making things happen, and am impressed now, as I recollect this, with the sense I seem to have had for the first time of power, of being able to do things, climb onto things, shout, throw things and walk around. It was a pure, vibrant and happy sense of simply being alive.

Stage one: Egocentric

Our memories usually begin when we go to school or slightly earlier. This is the beginning of Fowler's stage one, which normally runs from the age of about three years to about seven. Before that, our consciousness is relatively undifferentiated, something of a blur; but it is not unimportant because we are exposed to both painful and pleasurable experiences that will have an impact upon us. We are too young, though, to make any proper sense of them. We do not yet have the necessary thinking power and imagination.

In stage one, our experience is *egocentric*. We are at the centre of our world, and everything is self-referenced. We develop powers of imagination, but then have difficulty distinguishing what is real from what we have imagined. We usually have a strong sense too of omnipotence, of being able to control our environment in more or less the same way we control our arms and legs. If we want to stretch out our arms to reach something, we will it and it happens, more or less instantaneously. So it seems to be, at this stage, with everything else that we desire. The sense of power takes over. Likewise, we tend to try to simply will away everything we dislike.

Treating the world as an extension of ourselves is part of a primitive and immature psychological mechanism for dealing with desires and aversions, with our childhood likes and dislikes. In most cases, we have parent figures to guide us and set limits on what we get and what we do not, in addition to the natural limitations of childhood vulnerability, weakness, small stature, limited language and so on. In later years, however, people no longer make allowances, and we develop the muscular and intellectual strength to override unwanted restrictions. Carry over this style of interacting with the world into adulthood, though, and difficulties tend to multiply, both for us and for others. We risk becoming an impatient and unpopular kind of a tyrant.

This is why it is advisable not to indulge or spoil young children, giving in to all their wishes and desires, or helping them avoid everything that seems painful or difficult. The principle of growth through adversity is as important here as later. Self-discipline develops best in those who have learned restraint during childhood, as a result of their parents encouraging it in a kind and fair way. It is a form of 'tough love' imposed by those who know the value of self-discipline as an essential ingredient of sustained happiness and contentment. It involves learning to be satisfied with what you have. Only then can you discover true values and come to appreciate the meaning of generosity.

Discipline without love, on the other hand, can be highly destructive. Having your wishes denied repeatedly in such circumstances is likely to damage your sense of self-worth. It is worse still when your basic needs, including your needs for love, affection and praise, are consistently thwarted. Keith and Veronica's stories both remind us of that. Keith's father failed to deliver, as his grandfather had done before that. Veronica, raised in care homes and by unfeeling foster parents, had no contact with her real parents at all.

Not everyone, according to Fowler, moves on at the appropriate time from each stage to the next. Some get stuck for long periods in the early and immature stages. The kind of person who remains in stage one is rare, fortunately, but they can have important effects on the rest of us, for these are the types who evolve into arch-criminals, cult leaders and dictators.

Such people develop a kind of grandiose sense of omnipotence, devoting themselves utterly to achieving the outward manifestation of their inner sense of power and of being right, whatever the consequences to others. To put it simply, they operate through a combination of charm and deadly terror, for others are seen only as either expendable or ruthlessly to be exploited. Think again of the Nazi Party under Hitler, for example. The twentieth century saw the rise and demise of several such individuals, responsible together for tens of millions of deaths and unimaginable hardship throughout the globe.

Such dictators and similar people may well be thought of as embodying evil. However, we may be generous, and think of this as evil only in the sense of immaturity. If such people are indeed stuck developmentally in stage one, the implication is strong that they retain the possibility for further psychological growth. That seems hopeful, and there may be lessons here for detecting and managing such people within communities, although to discuss the subject at length is beyond the scope of this book.

Stage two: Conditioning

A child will usually begin moving into stage two at the age of six or seven years. Characteristically, such children love stories, and use narrative as their main way of understanding their experiences and giving them coherence. Ideally, in adulthood, we do not lose this, but develop it in tandem with testing reality more objectively and reliably. However, as children, we are likely to accept and adhere to stories, myths and symbols in a literal, rather than abstract, poetic or figurative way.

This is also the stage during which we learn about and become attached to the enduring stories, myths, beliefs, values and attitudes of our families and communities. They form a vital part of our emerging sense of our identities, of who we are. We may also pick up or be actively taught aversions to opposing or contradictory culture-based stories and belief systems, especially if we are raised in families or communities where conflict is endemic. These factors all form parts of our cultural *conditioning*, and will have to be transcended if we are later to make good progress on the spiritual path. This will mean giving up these learned and conditioned attachments and aversions, with all the attendant need for grief-work, catharsis and emotional renewal discussed in earlier chapters. For the most part, however, we carry these allegiances into the next stage, stage three.

Stage three: Conformity

There is no accurate timetable for movement from one stage to the next. There is overlap between the stages, and it may be best to think of them in terms of general descriptions rather than fixed categories. Stage three usually begins during the teenage years associated with adolescence. This is when we allow influences from outside the family circle to affect our thoughts, feelings and behaviour, or can no longer prevent the effects of these external factors.

We are exposed to such factors in the educational setting, in schools and later in colleges and universities, also through street culture, in the workplace, through the media, through religious organizations and so on. It is important to note, though, that stage three is an essentially *conformist* stage. During it, we are particularly well-tuned to the expectations, values and judgements of significant others, while remaining unsure of our own capacity to think and come to decisions for ourselves.

Even when involved in apparent teenage rebellion, we usually seek to conform to the rebellion group, realigning our allegiances according to the fashion of our peers in terms of clothing, hair styles, activities, music, sport preferences and team loyalties, for example. The new group remains essentially contained within the parent group. In a society geared up sensibly to contain it, we experience it as essentially safe. If problems arise, it is when a society is itself dominated by ambiguous and ambivalent adolescent values. Mature leadership is required. Reasonably disciplined social conventions – about honesty and trust, about family life, sexual behaviour, the use of intoxicants and about other important issues – are necessary too, to ensure the minimum of distress and the maximum of happiness within a community.

In stage three, we tend to hold powerfully and deeply to the beliefs and values we have acquired through conditioning in stage two. We do not yet have the occasion, ability or inclination to step outside these influences and examine them critically. We are unlikely even to be aware that we are holding to and living out a form of ideology.

This is the stage during which we conform and belong to a dualistic, 'us-and-them' culture. We are thus likely to be partisan, quick to judge and criticise others, simply on the basis of apparent or perceived differences. 'I do not like that person' is equivalent to saying 'I am not like that person'. What we are not aware of, during this still relatively immature stage of personal development, is the extent to which we use the defence mechanism of *'projection'* as a way of defending ourselves from anxiety and other painful feelings.

Projection arises when we deny aspects of ourselves that we would otherwise feel anxious, ashamed or guilty about. We are unconsciously protecting the idea "I am without fault". Having denied these negatively charged parts of ourselves, we project them into other people. The word comes from the Latin word 'iacio', which means 'I throw'. We are throwing out the unwanted bits to preserve the apparent purity of the ego.

This is where the split occurs, and where we usually lose touch with our true, spiritual selves, choosing an identity and adopting as real an incomplete 'persona' or mask. It is a fake-identity, fashioned for us largely by the conditioning we have received. This separation of everyday consciousness from the wholeness of the wisdom mind and from our true selves is the origin of the false ego-self. We accept it because we do not know any better at this stage, and have no way of knowing that who we think we are, how we think about ourselves and each other, is a kind of illusion. We accept as real the masks that everyone wears.

Carl Jung referred to the sum of the unacceptable cast-off aspects of each person's personality as the 'shadow', because it is always there, following us until we are ready to turn around, face and re-integrate it. Recognizing the split, healing it and making ourselves whole again will be the work of stages four and five. In the meantime, while still in the conformist stage, we dwell in a possessive world governed by attachment and aversion. We find ourselves dominated by ideas constantly related to 'I, Me & Mine'.

It is a world in which, continually fending off anxiety, shame and guilt, we have given ourselves a regular and significant problem. We have automatically produced opposition, and thus have all the trouble associated with confronting rivals and enemies. Projection is an unconscious mechanism, so we do not realize that we have created our foes. Neither do we realize *that they are exactly like us.*

Enemy may be too strong in this context, but it gives the essential flavour of the 'us-and-them' thinking at play, causing mischief and malevolence during stage three. We may not often actively oppose those we describe and think of as 'other'. After all, it may be risky to do so. However, neither do we usually engage with them in a friendly and co-operative fashion. We assume a kind of indifference and deem it acceptable. Analyse this indifference, though, and its essentially hostile origins quickly come to light.

Stage three is an adolescent phase, but adolescence can continue for a long time. According to Fowler's results, large numbers of any population will be in and working through the conformist stage, including about one-third of people in their fifties, and one-quarter of those over sixty. There is much to be learned to everyone's advantage by observing the mechanism of projection at work in ourselves and in others. We will surely understand, in time, individually and collectively, that here is the source of much conflict and human distress. More to the point, we discover *that conflict is largely avoidable* if we are able to grow a little wiser.

The attitudes and values inherent in stage three, conformist thinking are plainly inimical to human happiness. To be ruled by attachments and corresponding aversions, makes us favour rivalry and competition over co-operation. It makes us essentially defensive, protective of 'our' property and people, and quick to switch, when threatened, from defence to attack, from passivity to aggression and combat. We are also liable to prefer secrecy to openness, which at this stage will always seem potentially harmful towards our self-centred causes. We must accept as inevitable a way of life governed not only by mistrust and intolerance of others, but also by dishonesty; for it is as much of a lie to withhold truth as it is to spread falsehood.

Possessiveness naturally makes us desire to control people and situations. We seek power, and especially the power of wealth. Our values thus tend to be skewed towards those of commercialism. In itself, this may not be destructive, but we have already noted how commercial values can readily eclipse more wholesome spiritual values; competition, mistrust, secrecy, meanness, dishonesty and intolerance begin to hold sway over co-operation, friendship, openness, generosity, truth and open-mindedness. This is where real danger lies.

In order to grow beyond the conformist stage, a degree of soul-searching, of honest, contemplative self-appraisal is necessary. This eventually results in individuals taking responsibility for how they feel, rather than perpetually seeking someone else to blame and castigate, and from whom to seek recompense. But not everyone is yet ready to reflect in this way and discover wisdom.

Those still in stage three are not yet sufficiently emotionally ripe, so to speak. Those who have moved forward into the next stage often find this difficult to accept and contend with, as we shall see in the next chapter.

If, in the conformist stage, we were capable of honest self-awareness, we would recognize that what we always seek and endeavour strenuously to hold onto is a comfort zone. Our principal motivation is to find pleasure and avoid suffering. That is why we avoid drawing attention to ourselves as in any way different, because we may then fall victim to the projections of others, finding ourselves alienated, alone and under verbal or even physical attack.

There is safety in a kind of 'herd instinct', but there are also drawbacks. We must suppress our individuality, often painfully, by ignoring creative impulses. It is only possible to emerge from the crowd by adopting and adapting ourselves to socially sanctioned prescriptions. However, these formulae are unsatisfactory because they involve adhering to popular values of a superficial and transitory, essentially secular and materialist nature. These are adolescent values, not only those of power and wealth, but also of celebrity, beauty and fashion. They are unsatisfactory because genuinely creative impulses come from the true self, from the wisdom mind, the contemplative Sabbath mind, attuned to the sacred totality of the universe. To suppress this for the sake of conformity is to stifle something both precious and vital, the very sparks of life and healthy community.

I have no intention to criticize anybody, however it does seem worth emphasizing that there is harm and danger in taking relative worldly, secular values like these for incontrovertible absolutes. When sports and media personalities are referred to as 'icons' or 'idols', for example, this seems to indicate an absolute, even a religious degree of veneration. Too often, this is revealed as misplaced, when human limitations and failings are eventually exposed in the so-called 'iconic' figures. Idols, at least, are known to be man-made and fallible, but reference to them still causes absolute, spiritual values to be threatened with eclipse by those associated with worldly success, commercial advertising, consumerism and fashion. It is hard to avoid observing not only dishonesty at work, but an apparently widespread acceptance of dishonesty in secular culture. There is an inevitable price to pay: that of widespread mistrust.

These modern, transitory, adolescent and essentially self-centred values do not lead to lasting joy, much less to contentment for anyone. Associated with the seductive, secular idea of 'progress', they tend falsely to feed self-esteem. They feed regard for the incomplete mask, rather than the whole, true self. It does have an effect when people derive essential meaning and purpose in their lives from striving to belong to – and stay with – the group with which they identify: 'people like us'. But it leaves the pressing question of what can we do with the rest, with 'people not like us', with people we dislike? The answer, put simply, is threefold: to avoid them, to convert them to your way of life, or to destroy them.

None of these solutions is satisfactory. All three are difficult to achieve. More to the point, the real location of the problem is not in them but in us. This is why dictatorships fail. Even if we were to exterminate all our enemies, those into whom we have projected our shadowy parts, the true source of our distress remains unchanged. Unless we are able to recognize, accept this and mature, we will soon be looking around for new foes, including among our former friends and comrades. Transfer conflict from inside to out and it will never end. Understand ourselves, especially in terms of projection, in terms of emotions and the healing process, and we will have a better chance of finding both peace within and harmony with other people, even when at first they seem different and possibly hostile.

Projection does have an important psychological function. It prevents us from feeling stupid, anxious, afraid, ashamed, guilty or sad. At the conformist stage, we also tend to be strongly averse to uncertainty; so we are inclined to accede to authority and externally imposed discipline in public life, also to prefer dogmatic pronouncements supported by public institutions in fields such as politics, commerce, fashion, the media, science and religion. We tend to see things as black or white, with no in-between shades of colour or even intermediate greys. We are more comfortable joining together and letting others make decisions for the group. We do not always recognize that this might put us at the mercy of even less mature people, including dictators and similarly persuasive bullies. These organizers tend to offer strong leadership, not only through charm and by invoking fear, but also through concealment and dishonesty. They depend upon invoking intolerance within us towards others.

For such leaders to sustain their position, their psychological power and influence and their hold over us, they need an identified enemy. This is a shared foe, both to fear and to fight, someone made out to be so unlike us and so hostile to us that all we hold dear seems at risk. The threat is almost always exaggerated, because the 'enemy' is not so unlike us at all. In conformist stage three, however, we do not allow ourselves to see this. The emotion we are most comfortable with, because it conceals our fear and supports – albeit falsely – our sense of being in the right, is usually anger.

During stage three, we naturally prefer anger to fear and uncertainty. We feel better for actively resisting losses and threats, especially threats to self-esteem and to our strongly held beliefs and values. We may grow so accustomed to anger that we seldom conceive of it as a form of emotional pain. Paradoxically, even perversely, there are those who enjoy the sensation of anger. The angrier you feel, the easier it may be to convince yourself that you (and people like you) are strong and in the right; that your defiance is justified. Unfortunately for all concerned, this logic is simply false.

The thought patterns and emotional reactions of the conformist stage operate in the home, at work, in towns and cities, between and within communities and cultures, nationally and globally. They are worth learning to recognize, especially when at work in ourselves, for here we can do something about them. They are worth recognizing in others too. We may not be able to do as much about them there, but we can learn to try and protect ourselves from them, to minimize the misery and destruction they wreak upon us, and so set an example for others.

Commerce, politics and religion, in particular, infected by 'either/or', 'right/wrong', 'us-and-them' styles of thinking, quickly and inevitably result in conflict between people. Arguing and, worse, fighting over such deeply held sets of ideas and ideologies, serves only to entrench stage three people in their attachments and beliefs. It is hard to convert people's ideas. It is also hard to make personal progress from within the group.

The way forward will be in the hands of individuals. It involves each of us detaching ourselves from the original group identity, gradually letting go of our attachments to people, places, activities and the ideas with which we have previously identified. Remember it is not necessarily these things that we have to relinquish. It is the strength of our attachments to them. This is a subtle but important difference. It may not be easy. We often need some kind of push or incentive to change. It may take a crisis, an inescapable moment of decision, as it did the boy in Faulkner's Barn Burning story. This kind of forward movement, whether gradual or abrupt, heralds the change from the group conformism of stage three to the emerging individualism of stage four. This is where we must contend with new problems, as well as newfound joys and freedom. It is life beyond the comfort zone... the life of adventure!

Reflections

Are you independent-minded? In what ways can you be said to remain a conformist to the original ideals of your family, community and culture?

Do you tend to be a leader or follower of opinion? To what extent do you take responsibility for yourself, for the consequences of your thoughts, words and actions?

23. Avoiding Conflict and Chaos

Any weakness, viewed differently, can be seen as a strength and vice-versa. This is a key aspect of universal, 'non-dualist' thinking. The founders of the ancient Jain religion from India knew this principle and called it 'non-onesidedness'.

Jains are still teaching the wisdom of routinely reversing positive and negative attitudes as a foolproof way to get at greater wisdom and truth. Step into the other person's shoes. Envisioning matters from the perspective of anyone you oppose, improves the chances of friendship, of harmony and happiness for all.

Similar thinking is found among Taoists; that what strikes you first as negative turns out to have a positive side. Chuang Tsu tells, for example, about a town-dweller with a kypho-scoliosis, in other words a hunchback. This seems like a calamity and that the man is unfortunate, until it is pointed out in the story that he could still work at sewing and taking in laundry, winnowing and sifting grain, and so lacked nothing. In addition, he avoided conscription into the army and was given no work when a big public project was undertaken. He even received free grain and the firewood being handed out to the sick. The problem turned out to be a blessing in many ways.

Another view of democracy

We are wise, in similar vein, to seek the downside of whatever seems to have universal approval. Many communities are run by consensus or by representative groups, rather than by individuals. This works well and acts as a safeguard against ruthless tyranny. There are many good things to be said about democracy. Nevertheless, from another angle, there are flaws in it as a way of governing people, whether at a local or national level.

Democracy is based on the idea of contest, and is unavoidably dominated by 'us-and-them' thinking. A parliamentary democracy, like the judiciary system which supports it, is oppositional. However much co-operation between parties there may be behind the scenes, there are daily public confrontations, and so both winners and losers. Furthermore, such co-operation as does proceed is potentially self-serving and commercial rather than genuinely altruistic. Giveaway phrases used include 'bargaining' and 'doing deals'.

Ambitious people are likely to join, or form themselves into, political parties and seek election. In a society dominated by adolescent, secular and consumer values, people associated with wealth, power and celebrity tend to have the edge over those whose values are more mature and less materialistic. We have already noted the tendency of people at the conformist stage to seek the security of strong governance, rendering them vulnerable to dictatorial and other forms of partisan leadership. Democracy does not protect us from such one-sidedness. We are especially vulnerable to coercion when we feel under threat.

Firstly, the desire for reassurance of our own worth makes us susceptible to 'people like us' thinking. Secondly, our craving for safety makes us want secure, well-delineated and powerfully protected national boundaries and identities. Then, of course, we must defend them, aggressively if necessary.

Putting it bluntly, we are guided primarily by fear. This fear is the basis for anger. We naturally want both to get whatever we can and hold onto whatever we have. We grow angry with whoever seems to threaten that. Our sense of personal and collective vulnerability makes us feel needy and encourages us to be greedy. Research shows that increasing national wealth does not result in increased human happiness; but it seems to make no difference to know that. In fact, the research suggests that life just gets more stressful and therefore actually unpleasant; so we tend to elect those who persuade us that they can protect us from competition and conflict, and deliver just what we think we want.

The truth is that, under the guidance of our wisdom minds, *we want to be happy more than we want what we want.* Until we recognize this, anxiety is aroused more readily than admiration by alternative would-be leaders. Those who seek to appeal primarily to our wisdom and our humanity are much less popular than strong, partisan leaders. Politicians and others are not in favour who recommend tolerance, kindness and generosity towards those who seem different; for example, the poor, the sick and those with mental health problems, people from other cultures and faith traditions, and people from other countries who may not have enough food, healthcare, education and/or similar necessities. It takes maturity, and the wisdom of someone like Bridget, to see the intelligence involved in sharing what we have, allowing us to reap rewards from the gratitude and harmony this engenders.

Such fair-minded people are not only unlikely to be elected, but they are also less likely to seek office in the first place, wary of the duplicity, of the necessary intrigue and in-fighting likely to be involved. If they do seek to enter politics, there is difficulty at the beginning, joining and being adopted as a candidate by any political group or party, for these too tend to be defensive and accept only 'people like us'.

Democracy, then, makes it difficult for different, altruistic attitudes and values to emerge and become dominant, even though everyone is likely to be better off if they did. Change can occur though, and may already be occurring as we advance through social adolescence, away from the dominance of secularism towards spirituality, into a post-secular era. It begins with each of us, one by one.

Selfish, partisan and separatist thought patterns associated with the conformist stage of personal development obviously threaten to result in both conflict and social chaos. If there were no antidote, confrontation would be the norm. People would frequently have to take sides in defence of their friends and family, their property, their positions and their ideas. This is a recipe for general suspiciousness, for outright hatred and for full-scale war. Happily, however, the sun of wisdom has been shining on our forebears for countless generations.

One factor operating to prevent chaos in communities involves people deciding upon and enforcing a wise set of rules. Over the generations, *every* successful community – from small family to large nation – has devised or adopted a system of rules or laws to protect individuals and minority groups from exploitation and other forms of harm. These rules are not always stated explicitly, but where they are, they are remarkably similar throughout different cultures and throughout history.

Acknowledging spiritual government

The first and primary rule involves acknowledgement of a divine or sacred level of organization as the context for human existence. This is to admit and accept that there is something ultimate, consistent, absolute and incontrovertible about the way things work and happen. Recognition of such a dynamic and spiritually governed way of nature, referred to as the *Tao*, is at the heart of Taoism and of Zen. For many, the same principle implies the presence of a sacred and transcendent power or person, the ultimate arbiter, a deity called by many names, among them: God, Elohim, Allah, and Brahman.

To experience and come to accept at a personal level the ultimately divine nature of reality is also to discover that you are both commanded and inspired to submission and devotion. The first rule, to love God, takes care of itself in this way. Worship, gratitude and obedience follow naturally. Paradoxically, too, although the first rule is one of service, because our devotion is reciprocated and we may in turn feel loved by heavenly principle or a divine master, it is a rule which brings with it a general sense of freedom and release.

Even in a secular society, where science is the arbiter of knowledge and a supreme being or God is often denied, there is total respect for the rules we have conjectured about and discovered to govern nature. In physics, for example, we have both Newton's laws and quantum mechanics; an excellent example of how 'either/or' thinking has had to give way to the 'both/and' approach. In biology, we have the laws of genetics and a strong theory about evolution.

The five subsequent basic rules of successful communities are considered by many as the products of evolution, designed for survival and naturally worthy of respect. Even those without faith can respect their intelligence. Others do think them to be divine in origin. To obey them is seen as fulfilling a spiritual duty of sacred service. If inspired, we do so in the faith and security of knowing that these rules, received in a loving spirit, exist for our ultimate welfare.

After the first law, about loving and obeying God, the commonest remaining rules or guidelines involve five prohibitions:

Do not kill people
Do not steal
Avoid lying and dishonesty (especially if it is to gain advantage over or disrespect another person)
Avoid harmful sexual behaviour
Avoid excessive use of intoxicants like drugs and alcohol

These are the five principal precepts of Buddhism, for example, and are matched by several of the Ten Commandments of Judaism and Old Testament Christianity.

As guidelines for successful, harmonious living, these rules are well designed to combat the negative effects of conformist stage three thinking. Firstly, human life is considered sacred, of supreme value. Possessions are also highly valued, ensuring prosperity of the individual and also the group; but this is not the case if they have been attained through murder, theft or dishonesty. Theft means taking what has not been given freely, and so includes any form of exploitation or bullying. Lying includes withholding information as well as communicating falsehood, and this rule serves also to warn against disrespectful speech, gossiping, swearing and other potentially damaging forms of communication.

All five rules serve to protect and preserve the coherence and integrity of the group. Sexual misconduct may be defined strictly or liberally, either by individuals or the community. An important aim is to preserve family and communal structure, with obvious benefit to the community through protecting its most vulnerable and precious asset, its children. They should, ideally, be planned and wanted, and raised in an atmosphere of affection, love and discipline. This is good for everyone.

Intoxication, of course, increases the likelihood of breaches of the other rules. This is why it is proscribed, as well as to protect individuals from the risks and hardships attached to alcohol and drug abuse and dependence. In protecting individuals, the community is again protecting itself, in this case from the burden of sick, sorrowful, unproductive and needy members.

These rules make sense. In the egocentric stage, should it persist into adulthood, we are likely to ignore or flout them out of selfish self-interest. In the conformist stage, we are more likely to obey them; but, not through respect and devotion so much as through the fear of getting caught, of feeling ashamed, of losing status within the group, and of being punished. At the same time, still adolescent, we are likely to be ambivalent about rules that seem to spoil our chances of having fun, of getting pleasure and avoiding discomfort. Social conventions in contemporary Western culture concerning the use of drugs and alcohol, and about sexual behaviour, are extremely liberal and frequently flouted. This is immensely destructive in terms of human hardship and misery. It is worth considering whether this type of decadent behaviour can be understood in a positive way.

Keith eventually wanted to leave his job selling alcohol because of the negative effects it had on the people he saw 'out to enjoy themselves' in the pubs and night clubs where he worked. He saw people trying to escape their lack of personal fulfilment, and realized that alcohol did not relieve the problem; it made it worse. He saw people attempting to anaesthetize their distress, their anxieties and self-doubt, through intoxication; both legally with alcohol, and illegally with the provocatively (and perversely) named drug 'ecstasy' and similar substances. When discussing this, Keith also spoke to me of how often intoxication precedes loveless and promiscuous sexual activity, compounding rather than relieving personal shame and misery.

One explanation suggests that it is natural, during adolescence, to test ourselves against the rules and regulations set by our parents and by society. It may be better to explore the boundaries of possibility as you make decisions about what kind of person you are and want to be when relatively young, than to remain over-constricted by adhering rules out of fear. Nevertheless, the risk of getting trapped in destructively adolescent thought patterns and behaviour is high in a culture either failing to endorse the rules or, worse, promoting their contravention.

People receive ambiguous messages, for example, when the sale of one type of addictive and harmful intoxicant, such as heroin, is illegal and banned, while the widespread and intensive marketing of another type, alcohol, is clearly encouraged. Young people may even be the deliberate targets of some advertising campaigns. It is worth noting that in wiser cultures, intoxicants were introduced to the young specifically in the context of personal and spiritual development through ritualized initiation rites under close supervision. With secularism, few healthy rite of passage rituals remain, and growing up is much more haphazard.

In adolescent societies, dominated by the defence mechanism of projection, deep-seated fears about potential losses – of self-esteem, of possessions, of all that we hold dear – tend to prevail. Trust between people diminishes. We naturally look to political and other institutions for reassurance and protection. As a consequence, man-made rules tend to proliferate. These new laws grow more specific about and expand on the five basic rules governing people's behaviour towards each other and the community at large. They must then be both enforced and policed. The greater the level of fear in the community, the more rigorously the laws tend to be implemented and breaches punished. The more noticeable, too, are the exceptions where licence operates, such as regarding sexual behaviour.

There is a risk with strict policing, particularly when it some-times seems arbitrary, of contributing to a vicious cycle. As the laws and the policing of them get tougher, the level of trust between the populace and the institutions of society diminishes. People no longer feel in control of their lives. Whereas this suits many, others feel uncomfortably constrained. Some begin to protest legally. Some may both take the law into their own hands and encourage disobedience from others. To avoid social order breakdown, the surveillance and policing must become even more robust. It takes on a military, confrontational and even repressive demeanour. Civil liberties are further encroached upon. The revolving cycle of repression and disobedience inevitably gets cranked up. The general level of happiness in the community goes correspondingly down.

There are many possible negative consequences of such a situation. For example, the prisons fill up; but they do not necessarily function in the best way to reverse criminal behaviour back in the direction of good citizenship. Refugees fleeing hardship and persecution, many of them with much to offer by way of knowledge and skills, are resisted on the basis of suspicion and fear. Young people intuitively lose direction and motivation when they feel that their lives have been compromised by social and secular, rather than personal, creative and spiritual imperatives, and by social control. This can happen in democracies as well as in totalitarian states.

These observations, and many that are comparable, show how the conformist thinking patterns of stage three can go wrong, bringing about the very problems we fear and would all wish to avoid. Again, I am not judging or criticizing anyone here. It is not about taking sides or suggesting any kind of abrupt change. Social maturity will occur but will do so gradually, more likely on the scale of generations rather than lifetimes. We will, as national and international communities, grow wiser more satisfactorily and completely through a process of evolution than we could through any impatient, revolutionary attempt to force matters.

Leaving the comfort zone

Everyone goes through stage three. We all naturally want to protect what we identify with and feel to be ours. The best way forward, though, is not communally but one by one. Each must let go the strength with which we hold onto and defend some of our attachments; to grieve the associated losses, allow natural healing to occur, and in doing so mature emotionally as described in earlier chapters. Then, in the later stages of personal development, we will come to see and accept the wisdom of our basic rules, obeying them from choice in a relaxed and heartfelt way, knowing them to be appropriate and wise. In this we set an example for others to witness and follow.

Life's journey takes us from false, self-centred ego to the true self, to maturity and spiritual connectedness with the sacred whole. More than psychological and emotional development, this also represents growth towards faith.

Letting go of attachments and facing the accompanying painful emotions, especially the initial anxiety, requires faith. It requires a good measure of trust that things will turn out all right for us. We also require courage, to face the risk that matters may go wrong and bring pain. Such confidence and bravery as we can muster will depend on the degree of faith we have in the divine order of the universe and of human social relations. This faith, in turn, is the only possible author of hope; for we cannot rely on human institutions, operating on secular and materialist principles, unless these are subordinate to the sacred unity of the whole of humanity and the whole of the planet.

We cannot expect, however, to persuade people of this easily, people who remain governed by dualistic, conformist, 'right-or-wrong', 'us-and-them' thinking. Here is another story, a kind of parable, by way of explanation.

The sun is always shining, whether we see it or not. Two men lived with their tribe in a deep, hidden gorge tucked into the slopes of a steep mountain range close by the ocean. The geography of the place was such that a dense layer of mist hung perpetually over the steep-sided valley. The people dwelling there seldom encountered direct sunlight, living out their lives in twilight and gloom. One day, one of the men decided to break out, to seek his fortune elsewhere. This had happened before. In each generation, men had left the tribe; but none had ever returned.

The man tried to persuade a friend to accompany him, but the other would not leave the security of the tribe and the familiar terrain; so the adventurer set off alone. He had to climb steeply, travelling inland over high passes, through similar valleys, until by nightfall on the third day, after much doubt and difficulty, eventually following a watercourse, he had made his way down to a plain.

Waking the next morning, the traveller was struck by the clear sky, the bright sunlight, the brilliance of the colours around him, and the pleasant if unaccustomed force of the heat. It brought immediate joy to his heart. As he travelled on, meeting others, he noticed how much more cheerful they were compared with his own people. They were welcoming too. He could understand why no-one ever went back to the dark valley from which he had come. Life was so much better in the bright daylight; nevertheless, he remembered his friend. He made up his mind to return and persuade him to leave his comfort zone, to take the risk of leaving the valley and come to enjoy a much better life.

The man retraced his steps, following the watercourse back up into the mountains, returning over the high passes to the valley of his tribe. He was smiling when he again met up with his friend, but his friend was bewildered. He did not recognize this smiling man and mistrusted his words.

'The sun shines every day on the plain,' the man said. 'Everyone is happy and content. There is so much life, so much vivid colour. The crops grow in abundance. The animals grow fat. There is enough for all to share. The people are very well fed, and they are very friendly. Life is much less of a struggle. Why don't you join me? If you agree, we can come back again later and persuade others from the tribe to make the journey. Perhaps we can resettle everyone, and we will be hailed as heroes.'

In the event, the friend decided to stay. The man remained in the gorge for several weeks, trying to get him to change his mind; but only noticed himself growing frustrated and gloomy again. His friend could not conceive of and believe in the existence of a sun-lit country where people lived calm, happy lives of friendship and contentment. He remained convinced that he would be better off in familiar surroundings; so the man left his tribe once again. This time, he never went back. Eventually, the tribe diminished in numbers and finally disappeared.

This is a fanciful story, but it illustrates the journey we make as we leave the conformist stage and enter the more individual fourth stage of development. We have to leave others behind and do it alone. We leave them to their fate, which may be to perish; if not actually, then spiritually; because life cannot stand still.

It may be through simple but powerful curiosity, or it may involve a crisis, a brush with death or ruin, for example, or the need may dawn gradually, but many people do eventually come to question continuing membership of their group of origin. We choose, or are forced by circumstances, to re-examine the beliefs and assumptions about how things are and should be that we have been given. The next stage is one of individual and personal reappraisal of our conditioned attitudes and values. Leaving the comfort zone can be very positive and exciting, but it usually involves quite a challenge.

Reflections

Do you tend to be guided by caution or a spirit of adventure?

What would you do if you were the man's friend? Go with him or remain with the tribe?

---

24. Love, Sex and Maturity

Spiritual development, from adolescence towards maturity, can be summarized fairly simply. At stage three, we feel sure of our identities, *conforming* securely within our original family and communal group. At stage four, we begin to doubt and question our previous assumptions, rejecting some or most of them, beginning an *individual* search for greater wisdom and understanding.

At stage five, we find our way to a new level of *integration*, accepting holistic rather than separatist or partisan principles. We leave behind all the incomplete, false selves and identities assumed earlier as a result of our conditioning, and we begin wholemindedly to discover our true selves. We find ways of harmonizing with all people, and with the sacred, seamless unity of the whole universe. The group we are fully rejoining is humanity. Completing the process in stage six, we will marry all personal agendas with that of fostering universal well-being. By both example and precept, we will take naturally to *teaching* what we have learned. Our natural inclination will be towards *healing* where distress and damage are found.

A second important factor promoting peace and harmony, preventing social conflict and chaos, involves each one of us working towards maturity as individuals. This necessarily supplements the adoption and enlightened enforcement of a set of wise rules. Not everyone in power is a tyrant. Some leaders are wise, mature and benevolent, wanting to make use of guidance from the ripened perceptions of others as well as their own insights and experience. Their aim will be the happiness of the people, and they will recognize the primary importance of virtue, above that of either security or prosperity, in achieving and maintaining that target. Other psychologically and morally mature people will be content to remain unnoticed, but will also exert a strong influence for the good of the community. Living holy lives, they set the rest of us an example.

These wise people will first have emerged from the group and the conformist stage, demonstrating the ability to think for themselves. Any move made forward into the individual stage, stage four, is critical. It is like a new awakening to oneself as a separate being, free to make choices and accept responsibility for the consequences of whatever we intend, think, say and do (likewise for whatever we do not think, choose not to say and avoid doing). We must begin, however, with a warning.

A state of transition

Remember the valley-dweller who discovered a better place where the sun shone, returning to his friend and his tribe to tell them about it. He remained with them for many weeks, trying to convert them to his new vision, but they were not ready. This man was in a transition phase, and was at risk of getting stuck there; neither in the parental group, nor free of it. Reasoning did not work. Pleading with people was equally useless. Sometimes he grew angry, and tried to remonstrate with friends and family, but he discovered this too to be counter-productive.

We could call it 'stage three-and-a-half' when someone grows dissatisfied with the parent generation's edicts and restrictions, the partial myths and false assumptions, the 'us-and-them' logic behind prevailing attitudes and many decisions, the security-mindedness, possessiveness and protectionism, the underlying anger and fear. Many of us, however, like the valley-dweller, come to the conclusion that somehow we need to change the existing regime. We may even begin thinking in terms of rebellion and revolution.

The warning mentioned above is a reminder that we are still affected by the psychological defence mechanism of projection. Accordingly, we identify in members of our own former group traits that we have begun to recognize as problematic in ourselves. It does not work, however, to be intolerant of intolerance, to reject rejection, or to join a partisan group that resists a partisan philosophy in others. These tactics can only serve to perpetuate tension with the prevailing order, which strengthens its resistance against us and our new ideas. In the struggle, we may overcome and forget our fears and anxieties, but we risk being dominated by newly acquired or amplified frustration and anger in the face of intolerance and injustice.

However righteous and justified it may seem, anger is always destructive in nature. Tolerance, wisdom, understanding and love inform wiser and more successful strategies.

Fighting for peace, for example, if the words are taken literally, cannot be expected to work. On the contrary, fighting for anything leads directly to conflict and human suffering. As our efforts against the leadership regime seem to fail, so might we grow disillusioned and be at risk of despair. We might feel guilty at not trying harder, and ashamed at our lack of success. Perhaps we redouble our efforts for a while, but eventually find ourselves turning away exhausted, in doubt and confusion. There must be another way, we might think, and pause wisely for reflection.

In the end, though, the man from the dark valley could only let go of his ambition to convert his friend and his tribe, grieve for them and sorrowfully go on his way.

If, alternatively, our efforts – revolutionary or democratic – happen to be successful in supplanting the former ruling group, our problems are not over when we take control or become part of a new administration. Wherever power is held, whether in families, in the community, in commercial, political, religious or other organizations, projection remains a powerful factor. Members of the new group no longer necessarily hold to the same agenda, and may quickly split into factions. Even if the ruling group does manage to remain reasonably united, there will soon be new opposition from elsewhere: from dissatisfied group members, constituents or shareholders. Defensive philosophy and partisanship inevitably surface again.

Pausing for reflection

Will we go on fighting, or move on? This is a dilemma, a personal crisis, a time for decision. Like the boy in the barn-burning story, we must find and follow a new destiny and enter life's stream alone; only then will we have genuinely embarked on stage four. We now have the chance to become individuals on the road to personal integrity, wholeness and spiritual health, in search of mature love, happiness and our true selves. It is a good time to pause again for reflection. Contemplation is helpful. Here is what Thomas Merton once wrote on the subject:

Contemplation is the highest expression of man's intellectual and spiritual life. It is that life itself, fully awake, fully aware that it is alive. It is spiritual wonder. It is spontaneous awe at the sacredness of life, of being. It is a vivid realization of the fact that life and being in us proceed from an invisible, transcendent and infinitely abundant Source. Contemplation is, above all, awareness of the reality of that Source. [35]

Climbing out of the gorge, travelling on foot through the wild country of the high mountain passes, discovering a stream and following it down to the plain, the tribesman of the story began to notice his solitude and experienced a sense of loneliness. His surroundings were unfamiliar. He did not know what dangers might be lurking. He felt ill-equipped, and was appropriately anxious. His faith and courage held, however, and he soon found good new circumstances and, importantly, a generous welcome from people on the plain.

Stage four: Individuality

The fourth stage of development, during which we differentiate ourselves from our original family and communal group, may or may not involve travel, but it does involve distancing ourselves mentally from people and places of former attachment. We are leaving behind our comfort zones, and must expect difficult situations and painful feelings. It is particularly difficult if, for

---

[35] From *New Seeds of Contemplation* by Thomas Merton. See 'Recommended Books and Websites'.

example in a marriage or other form of intimate friendship, one partner moves forward at a faster pace than the other, or in a slightly different direction. It might seem like a betrayal of love.

Sex, romance and relationship

During adolescence, when we discover our appetite for sex, we tend to indulge and express it according to prevailing family and cultural conventions. If a pair-bond relationship is to form when two people meet, sexual attraction plays a large part. Sexuality involves strong feelings of attachment, to the point where we might even hear a person say 'I love sex'. For such people, their attachment is to erotic activity itself. This becomes destructive whenever it takes precedence over the desire to form genuine and respectful human relationships. The attachment becomes an addiction. In healthier situations, attachment behaviour is directed towards another person in the hope of mutual friendship.

As we begin learning about possible partners and perhaps experimenting with them, there is a romantic link between love and sex. The novelty and power of the feelings, the intrusive intensity of our thoughts about our sex partner of the moment, captivate us. We naturally think we are in love, and that it will last forever. This, for example, is how it was between June and Ron when they met. However, this form of love is partly illusory. It can be considered immature when it involves a degree of self-seeking. There will be an element of possessiveness, also an imbalance in terms of dominance and control. The main emphasis of this kind of love is physical or, rather, *biological.*

The drive towards pair-bonding during adolescence gets our

attention and makes us think. It makes us reflect on who we are and what we want; and so is a powerful force in propelling us towards maturity. Loving and losing a partner; to a rival, through separation or because of diminishing interest; is a common experience. Nevertheless, as we have seen, emotional release permits healing. We can grow stronger and wiser with each loss.

As relationships develop, *psychological* factors supersede the biology of sex in keeping couples together. After meeting a suitable partner, it is symbolic of entering adulthood when we then make our commitment to the relationship public. This may be a formal type of engagement, followed by marriage, or it may just involve openly cohabiting. Either way, including families, friends and members of our community in the relationship process brings the *social* dimension into play too.

Making a commitment to pair-bonding for life also takes on *spiritual* significance. The bond may or may not be recognized as extending into eternity, but weddings traditionally involve religious ceremonies during which the most sacred vows are publicly under-taken. God, the sacred unity, is often called upon in prayer as a witness and to act as guarantor for the union. All present may be expected to respect that, and help the couple maintain their vows.

This attitude is not common in a predominantly secular society, even where marriages are still conducted in the context of religious services. Kelly and Brett's is an example of a modern relationship. Couples like this, meeting in their twenties when they are no longer sexually naïve, are usually drawn together partly by sexual attraction, partly by shared interests and compatible values. If they share in a crisis, such as Kelly's unwanted pregnancy forced upon her and Brett, it can steer the relationship into a more adult form as they weather it together. Problems and crises like this are threatening, but they can also act as cement, strengthening bonds between people.

With time, mature relationships between couples tend to depend less on passion and sexual desire. They are more evenly-balanced friendships, in which the two people have been able to subordinate themselves and surrender to one another totally. Sex remains important, but the focus of erotic behaviour changes from primarily self-gratification in the direction of mutual pleasure. Perhaps surprisingly, it was the Cistercian monk, Thomas Merton, who wrote of married couples:

The act of sexual love should by its very nature be joyous, unconstrained, alive, leisurely, inventive and full of a special delight, which the lovers have learned by experience to create for one another. [36]

This kind of love can be blissful, transcendent. In a responsible, committed, loving and sacred partnership between two people, there is in sex a spirit of celebration, gratitude, joy and purity; but if a couple are to stay together happily through the middle years and into old age, the two partners must both mature. Instead of being the 'other half' of each other, they can gradually become a dyad made of two wholes. No longer, as it were, facing each other, oblivious to the world around them, they grow increasingly awake

---

[36] From *Love and Living* (p117). See 'Recommended Books and Websites'.

to the plight of others, and so travel on through life side by side. The sharing of values involves developing spiritually, as well as socially and emotionally. These three aspects go together. Although some couples do stay together through sharing 'us and them', partisan values; it is arguable that they do so less happily than those who treat other people as equals, with honesty, tolerance and kindness.

Deepening love

In a successful couple, both partners acquire spiritual skills, ideally through the sharing of spiritual practices. The highest and most mature form of love in relationships is thus reliably associated with happiness, with the pain-free side of the emotional spectrum: with joy, innocence and contentment; with freedom from confusion, doubt, anger, guilt and shame. We can recognize this maturity of love by its honesty, purity and spontaneity. Mature love makes things whole. It balances opposites and resolves all ambivalences. In this sense, the mature love between two people mirrors the universe. It is a reflection of the cosmic whole.

Kelly and Brett eventually decided to have a family. This is the basic purpose of sex in nature, that of procreation. Parental love then grows out of marital love. Love quite literally breeds love – a love that grows, expands, broadens and deepens, enveloping more and more people: first family and close friends, then acquaintances, eventually strangers and even apparent enemies. This is the nature of genuine, mature, selfless, communal, spiritual love.

Children, like Bridget, born into loving marriage partnerships thrive emotionally; whereas those like Veronica, June and Keith, born to ambivalent, loveless, transient or failed relationships, tend to struggle with life from the outset. They have greater difficulty discovering or creating meaning and a sense of purpose, because they often feel unloved, unloving and unlovable. It is a greater challenge for such people to find love and happiness, but it is not impossible. Many have succeeded and there is always hope of healing these, the earliest and deepest of emotional wounds.

'Love is patient. Love is kind,' says St Paul in his first letter to the Corinthians, (chapter 13, verses 4-8). 'Love is not envious or boastful or arrogant or rude. It does not insist on its own way; it is not irritable or resentful. It does not rejoice in wrongdoing, but rejoices in the truth. It bears all things, believes all things, hopes all things, and endures all things. Love never ends.'

St Paul is here describing the pinnacle of mature love as manifest in relationships, in families and throughout thriving communities. This kind of sacred love celebrates differences as well as similarities. It knows no envy, rejoicing always in the good fortune of others. It will heal us and protect us from harm and despair. It joins us intimately, one to another and to nature, to creation. It is that for which we all search, and of which we already carry within us the seeds. Love is our true nature. Root out self-seeking, passion, desire and hatred, and love will be revealed.

When we die, we will be forced to let go. We must give everything back. We will retain nothing – except love. Travelling on, we follow increasingly faithfully the guidance of the Sabbath, of our wisdom minds. As we near the end of our pilgrimage, we will become mature in love. As we negotiate the different stages of spiritual development, love will be our prize. At the end, as with my

Grandfather, the legacy we bequeath to the future, the shining reflection of our true selves, will be love.

Reflections

What are the dangers of trying to convert others to your way of thinking?

Have you ever felt stuck doing this, when the effort is great but the response is poor or uncertain?

Where are you on the pathway to love and maturity? Does it help to think that you may need to grow and mature further, and that it can be acceptable to leave others in relative darkness until you are wiser and stronger?

25. Approaching Perfection, Becoming Whole

The critical move towards spiritual maturity involves leaving the group. When we go from the conformist into the individual stage of development, the first signal from our wisdom minds may be a growing sense of discomfort and dissatisfaction with the way things seem to be going, both personally and in the world around us. We may initially become aware of the change, and that we are called upon now to make an adjustment in our philosophy and way of life, when we start feeling particularly lost, lonely and out of place.

It seems important to be able to recognize this step as a natural part of the process of transition from one stage to another, and not dismiss it as a form of psychiatric symptom, for example, or feel guilty and try to hide and deny it. It involves finding the wisdom to feel good about feeling bad for a while, during the period of transition.

Sigmund Freud was a great thinker and writer, but he left an unfortunate legacy whereby his work led people to consider the unconscious as somehow dark and threatening, containing masses of shameful and frightening material that was hard to get at, hard to make sense of, and harder still to come to terms with. Unlike Carl Jung, Freud also seems to have dismissed spirituality and he devalued religion. It is time to revise these attitudes, which naturally make people wary and tend to discourage us from engaging whole-mindedly and wholeheartedly with the unconscious, as we must in order to find healing and make spiritual progress. Kelly's unconscious was full of grief when she came to see me, as was June's, but both were able to grow and mature through facing the emotional pain instead of trying to ignore or bury it again.

Some growing pains are inescapable. This is akin to the shedding of layers, the skins of previous conditioning, and it leaves us temporarily vulnerable as we develop. It is like the transformation of the slow-moving caterpillar and the emergence of a beautiful butterfly. The ancient Greek word for butterfly – *psyche* – we use for both mind and soul.

Something, some event or series of happenings, some idea or set of ideas, will have woken us up; whether suddenly or gradually; to see important aspects of our lives as no longer wholly true and acceptable. Our traditional beliefs and values, our relationships, the way of life we have adopted and shared with our families and communities all come to seem incomplete, flawed and empty of meaning.

Perhaps we have been affected by moving away from home, like the valley-dweller in the story, meeting people from different backgrounds with different traditions and lifestyles. If they are not friendly, or we are overly suspicious of these apparently alien folk, we may not be able to relax immediately, feel we belong, find a new home and more meaningful way of life. We must sometimes be prepared, then, to continue our quest.

It is sadly true that we may remain uncomfortable, lonely and unhappy, stuck for a long time at the individual stage and in the time of transition to the next stage of integration. It is especially likely if we have learned to reject but not yet to affirm. In rejecting, we feel rejected. In failing to affirm, we never ourselves feel affirmed. This leads to a kind of spiritual malaise, resulting from failure to connect properly with the positive life force imbuing the sacred whole of the universe. We may even be in denial that any such mysterious source of vital energy exists or can exist, especially when this has not yet been a direct part of our experience.

The way forward involves opening ourselves up whole-mindedly to new experiences, new teachers and new possibilities. We need others, people who have reached stages five and six, themselves familiar with and highly influenced by the holy spirit of the universe, to show us the way. What we need, above all, is to experience acceptance and love.

Do you remember how something like this happened to June? The energy and laughter of children in the home where she worked stirred something dormant within her, which was then kindled further into life by Sam's love and that of his children. Eventually, under the divine influence of love, compassion and wisdom, we too can reach a new and expanded feeling of belonging, of being at home in our new circumstances. Then we will discover new, universal values through an enriched level of understanding. We will come to realize that 'everyone's blood is red, and everyone's tears are salty'. The similarities between people far outweigh the differences. Our new group, into which we eventually feel fully integrated, will be the whole of humanity.

Stage 5 Integration

Making such discoveries is how we begin the integration process of stage five. We are all vulnerable and (as discussed in chapter 3) have identical basic needs. It will eventually become plain to us that these will be met more readily and satisfactorily through co-operation, rather than through treating the people we encounter as rivals for limited resources. We can already see that this is potentially an excellent recipe for happiness, our own and everyone else's, but fear and greed may yet prevent us from committing to it.

It will take a breakthrough into universal consciousness, like a Zen 'kensho' or my own transcendent experience facing the reality of extinction through solving my Grandfather's riddle, to give us the new and necessarily enlightened global perspective. This new, mystical vision reveals incontrovertibly that each of us is an inseparable part of the sacred whole. We are likewise shown seamlessly connected to each other, according to what the Buddhist master Thich Nhat Hanh has called 'Interbeing'[37]. Everyone is experienced as intrinsically valuable and worthy of love; those once considered our opponents included. Recognizing the power of reciprocity, which means that whatever we do to another equates with doing it to ourselves, we can no longer conceive of people as enemies, much less oppose and fight against them.

Peace will begin its reign in our hearts during the integration phase, but this is not yet the end of our journey. There may be further struggle before we attain maturity, lasting happiness and contentment. For example, we may no longer think of others as enemies, but this does not prevent some people from seeing us as some kind of a threat. We will need to learn to deal with that

---

[37] Thich Nhat Hanh is the author of a number of useful books about mindfulness. See 'Recommended Books and Websites'.

harmoniously, and we will still have residual immature, self-seeking tendencies to contend with and convert. We may also have a legacy of destructive past actions to accommodate psychologically, and will want to make reparation where possible.

Tasks of personal development

The twelve-step method for managing addictions, pioneered by Alcoholics Anonymous[38] has been adopted by similar organizations for drug addiction, gambling and other problems. Those familiar with these steps will recognize the tasks pertaining to personal development. Addiction, like Veronica's to jackpot machines, for example, is an extreme form of attachment; so the twelve-step principles can reliably be expected to be appropriate and useful for everyone to consider. They seem relevant particularly to stages four and five, because at stage three we are not yet likely to be ready to commit ourselves to enduring discomfort in the interests of growth. Some form of spiritual awareness is necessary, and underpins the individuation and integration processes. We will need to tap into the sacred source of moral strength to undertake and make progress on our journey. This idea resonates closely with the twelve steps, which can be adapted and written as follows:

Steps 1 & 2: acknowledgement

I admit that I am powerless over certain strong attachments and aversions, and have come to believe that a sacred unity, a power

---

[38] The AA website is listed in 'Recommended Books and Websites'.

greater than myself, could restore me to psychological health.

Step 3: a decision is made

To turn my will and my life over to the care of this Unity, Power, Higher Consciousness or God, as I understand Him.

Commitment to such a decision is deeply personal. It is usually made, and can only be enduringly effective, when a person entering the individual stage has negotiated a crisis of conscience brought on by their suffering. We have already noted (in chapter 15) a link between crises and making key life decisions. After commitment, progress can be made through the following steps, which also involve decisions:

Steps 4 & 5: further decisions

To make a searching and fearless moral inventory of myself; also to admit to my God, to myself, and to another human being the exact nature of my wrongs and defects of character.

Step 6: recognition

I am entirely ready to seek completion, and for all these defects of character to be healed.

Step 7: a humble request in the form of a prayer

For healing, to remove my shortcomings.

Steps 8 & 9: more decisions

To make a list of all the persons I have harmed, and to make direct amends to such people wherever possible.

Buddhists and others familiar with *karma*, with what is described as 'the law of cause and effect', will recognize the need for this reparatory work and the benefits it will give. Recognizing our shortcomings and making amends will be essential to our integration with the community of our origin and the new global community.

These steps resonate equally with Christ's commandments 'to love God, and your neighbour as yourself'. They follow the same logic as the Sermon on the Mount, which demonstrates remarkable psychological as well as spiritual insight. Here are some examples.

"First take the log out of your own eye, and then you will see clearly to take the speck out of your neighbour's eye" (St Matthew chapter 7, verse 5), is about projection. "Do not store up for yourselves treasures on earth... but store up treasure in heaven" (St Matthew chapter 6, verses19 - 20), is a poetic way of emphasizing spiritual over secular values, and recognizes that worldly attachments are the inevitable precursors and causes of emotional pain. "If anyone strikes you on the right cheek, turn the other also" (St Matthew chapter 5, verse 39), demonstrates a clear grasp of the principles of 'interbeing' and reciprocity.

It is particularly during the integration stage that we may benefit from reading such inspired and inspirational texts, from Christianity and from other world faiths. We are better prepared to understand and make use of their deepest meanings, and it no longer matters whether we consider ourselves adherents to a particular tradition. It does not even matter if we have rejected formal religion entirely; although many do find a new enthusiasm for traditional ritual and worship. Many find their way back to a religion they thought they had left behind, seeing it with new eyes.

We are newly primed, during stage five, to receive spiritual wisdom and truth, finding ourselves filled frequently with profound feelings of joy, inner peace, frequently accompanied by a sincere gratitude that makes us want to give something back.

Proceeding successfully through the integration stage, gaining fresh insights, we begin naturally to take responsibility for our attitudes and values, for our personal lifestyle and beliefs. We begin both to make new commitments and importantly to honour them. Whenever these lead us into tension with others, we see things more easily from their point of view and become naturally more diplomatic. We will no longer hold quite so tightly to our attachments to people, possessions and ideas, and will feel correspondingly free. No longer interested in winning or losing arguments, our aim is not exactly to heal the past. It is more about healing the present, and preparing ourselves and others for a more harmonious future. The remainder of the twelve steps reflect all this, as follows:

Steps 10 & 11: further decisions

To continue to take a personal inventory, and when I am wrong, promptly to admit it.

To seek through prayer and meditation to improve my conscious contact with God, as I understand Him, praying only for knowledge of His will for me and the power to carry that out.

Step 12: final decisions to pass on wisdom and teach by example. [B]

Having had a spiritual awakening as the result of these steps, to try and carry the message to other people, and to practice these principles in all my affairs.

These points recognize the need to remain self-aware and to persist in a deliberately mindful connection with the infinite. They recognize too that our happiness is bound up with that of others.

Stage 6: Becoming whole

In the integration stage, we will become increasingly compassionately aware of human suffering around us, and we naturally want to help relieve it. We must learn, however, that compassion without wisdom leads to exhaustion, and so be careful to maintain our own physical, psychological and spiritual health. We will do well to seek the support of similar spiritually-minded individuals, who we tend to recognize readily and intuitively because neither they nor we are wearing false masks.

Resolving our ambivalences, facing and growing through pain, we no longer need to wear such a mask for protection. After the healing processes of lysis and catharsis have taken effect, emotional energy is now freely available, leaving us more expressive, creative and spontaneous. Our greater levels of resilience and equanimity make us better company, and better equipped to accompany, support and comfort others in their distress.

The process of integration, of becoming whole, may take a long time. It also necessarily involves facing the reality of our own death and the threat of extinction. This may well be difficult; but increasingly free of personal suffering, more compassionately aware of the distress of others, our thoughts will also turn naturally to passing on whatever wisdom we think we have found.

As with other transitions between stages on life's journey, there is no clear-cut delineation between stage five and the teaching and healing stage that follows. Few people achieve stage six early enough to be recognized as spiritual masters, and, in a secular society, they are relatively unlikely to be identified. Nevertheless, Mother Teresa of Calcutta, Martin Luther King, the Dalai Lama, Thich Nhat Hanh and Thomas Merton are all candidates from within living memory. I can personally vouch for the Dalai Lama[39], Nhat Hanh and, in particular, Merton; and I suspect that among us there are very many other living saints, ordinary people quietly living holy lives, lives of wisdom, compassion and joy.

As humanity proceeds, generation by generation, we can confidently anticipate fewer people being left behind in the earlier stages of spiritual development. Greater numbers will proceed further towards wisdom and maturity. Humanity is going through a kind of adolescent period. The pain and uncertainty involved, however, will stimulate increasing numbers to emerge from the group. It will be like when you heat water and increasing numbers of molecules vaporize, until it is all eventually boiled off as steam. More and more people will break away from the group and begin seeking their way as individuals towards perfection and integration. As humanity, we will evolve, generation by generation, by gradually improving our capacity for a holistic or 'wholeminded' approach to life and to each other.

As the balance of numbers shifts preponderance from the

---

[39] His Holiness the Dalai Lama kindly endorsed my book *Happiness: The 30 Day Guide*, written under my pen name. See 'Recommended Books and Websites'

earlier stages towards stages four, five and six, so the pendulum will swing. The mass of humanity will move towards a potentially rapid sea-change. As more people engage in spiritual practices and develop spiritual skills, the more mature individuals will increasingly affect their communities and society at large. Institutions like those of health care, mental health care and education are ripe for this kind of conversion. As secular values and principles diminish, we can hope for and expect commercial organizations and political institutions eventually to follow.

As mature, selfless and spiritual values assert themselves, we will increasingly discover and adhere to Bridget's recipe for contentment: cultivating loving and trusting friendships; taking each day as it comes; being grateful for what we have; sharing it freely, however little; thinking, speaking and acting with kindness and compassion; being honest, especially with ourselves; being tolerant and accepting our limitations.

As the balance is gradually restored between spirituality and secularism; with universal co-operation taking priority over divisive competition where they clash; love, healing and happiness will surely prevail. That, anyway, is my hope.

Reflections

This is the final page. Every ending is a new beginning...

Now, it is over to you...

Are you ready?

APPENDIX ONE
Universalist Religions

Everyone should be taught to meditate during childhood, and everyone should have two religions. These are the thoughts of a friend who is an Anglican priest. Shared spiritual insights emerge through meditation, he says, and the key tactic is to seek similarities and areas of compatibility, rather than differences and points of dispute.

Show allegiance to more than one faith tradition and you will have at least two angles from which to fix your position on the great map of world theology. You will have a greater range of scripture from which to draw wisdom and inspiration, and a wider set of beliefs and practices from which to choose to engage. You will also belong to a much larger faith community, from which to obtain guidance and support. As we emerge from the grip of dualist, black and white, right and wrong thinking, these ideas make excellent sense.

In calling myself a 'Universalist' Christian, I mean that Christianity is my parent faith, which I continue to practice, also that I am open to the teachings and practices of other world religions. I respect the spiritual truths at the heart of each faith and feel great kinship with their devotees. I enjoy harmonious religious discussion, love sacred music from many sources, and similarly love going to synagogues, mosques, temples, monasteries, cathedrals, churches and all manner of places of worship. In all this, I take my cue from Thomas Merton.

I am also sensitive to the spirituality of morally minded non-believers, agnostics and atheists. What we share vastly outweighs what seems to separate us. We have the same needs, and are engaged in the same struggle not only to survive but also to find meaning and a sense of purpose in our lives.

I therefore encourage people to accept this label – 'Universalist' – using it solely as an adjective, and wearing it lightly. This will give us 'Universalist' Jews and 'Universalist' Muslims, as well as 'Universalist' Christians. It means other styles of 'Universalist' faiths too: 'Universalist' Hindus, Buddhists, Jains and Sikhs, for example.

It is true that Hinduism and Buddhism can already, in their unique ways, be considered universalist belief systems. They both tend to be inclusive, either absorbing other faiths or accepting parity with them. They are essentially non-oppositional traditions; and Sikhism was similarly founded by Guru Nanak specifically to bring harmony between Muslim and Hindu. The Baha'i tradition is also already openly universalist, in that it emphasizes the unity of humankind and its religions, seeking world peace.

Widespread adoption of this unifying philosophy seems appropriate at this conflict-ridden time in world history when mistrust frequently prevails between citizens, communities, countries and cultures. Agnostics and atheists might even think about calling themselves 'Universalist' too. Meeting each other, Universalist people from all faiths and none will have much to share and much to rejoice over. When trust is established between them, wisdom, peace and happiness will flourish. All manner of things will be well.

APPENDIX TWO

Reflection on the word 'Jihad'

The word 'jihad' is Arabic. It means religious warfare, specifically a war for the propagation or defence of Islam. In recent times, it has strong connections with violent conflict and terrorism; but it does have other meanings.

I am grateful to medical student Naeema Rashid, a Muslim, for pointing out in her essay on spirituality and health that in Arabic 'jihad' can mean 'fight', but equally 'effort' or 'struggle'. She wrote of the struggle a patient sometimes gets into with his or her illness as a kind of personal jihad. The way forward for a Muslim is through submission to the will of Allah, the word 'Islam' meaning exactly that: 'submission'. The will of Allah, of God, is often difficult both to discern and comply with, hence the occasion for effort and struggle. The location of this struggle, this jihad, is primarily within you. Doctors, other health care workers and your own supporters do well to appreciate and respect that. You will have no wish, and limited energy, to struggle with them as well.

These ideas also fit in with the discussion in this book about personal growth in stages towards spiritual maturity. In the *conformist* stage and earlier, our jihad will be aimed at others from outside our original community, at people we consider our opponents and enemies. Later, becoming dissatisfied and increasingly at odds with the parent group's traditional ideology and customs, the effort and struggle to detach ourselves involves turning our jihad in a new direction. We now oppose and may be opposed by family, friends and other upholders of the original tradition.

In time, entering fully into the *individual* stage of development in search of our true nature, we see through and learn to relinquish the psychological defence of projection. We no longer seek out, judge and try to convert perceived shortcomings in others that tend to mirror our own. We start taking full responsibility for self-improvement according to spiritual ideals. A Christian may recognize the determination and effort required to 'take up the cross', giving up selfish pursuits in the hope and expectation of redemption. A Buddhist will understand similarly the wisdom of engaging energetically with karma in the search for enlightenment. From a psychological perspective, the 'jihad' during this stage is deeply personal, involving playing out – as in a drama – the opposition between our true and false selves. At the mercy of strong remaining dislikes and desires, the inner contest may feel as if we are struggling either with God or with Satan. This kind of imagery is more or less universal. Invoking angels against demons, it can work even for non-believers.

When we eventually learn the wisdom of submission to the divine benevolence of nature, the combined processes of healing and growth foster maturity. As we enter the *integration* stage, less effort is required and our struggles begin to resolve. The jihad is not over, but in sensing a successful outcome, we may already begin to feel liberated. A new kinship with and love for humanity arises in our hearts. Happiness is securely within our grasp as, healers and teachers now, we turn our final, more enlightened jihad outward once again, intent on the benefit of all.

Acknowledgements

First thanks and acknowledgements go to my many patients over the years, particularly those whose stories appear in these pages.

I am immensely grateful to John Hunt for commissioning this book, and for helpful comments with the text. My thanks are due also to Florence Hamilton for her excellent editing and to Judith Kendra at Rider Books for advice with earlier titles. I owe much to Stuart Johnson for help formulating many of the ideas here about spirituality, particularly in the context of health care, and to Andrew Powell for encouragement and for helping me find the right words.

Precious teachers, guides, spiritual friends and long-term meditation partners, living and dead, have included Theresa and Billy Andrews, Joe Bartlett, Scott Brusso, Ruth and Terry Clarke, Annie Cousins, Sarah Eagger, Fiona Gardner, Patrick Jansen, Mary Nathan, Tony Pannett, Paul Quenon, Paul Rampton, Elizabeth Waddy, Emmy Weisters, Kenneth Wilson and quite a few anonymous others.

Friends who have generously allowed me the peace to write in seclusion on their properties at different times include Stephanie and Sherwood Elcock, Zakia and Charles Powell.

I am most grateful to all.

Extracts are reprinted with permission as follows:
Zen and the Brain by James H. Austin, MD, MIT Press.
New *Seeds of Contemplation* by Thomas Merton, copyright
©1961 The Abbey of Gethsemani, Inc., New Directions

Publishing.

Love and Living by Thomas Merton, Farrar, Strauss & Giroux (applied for).

Man's Search for Meaning by Viktor Frankl, Beacon Press (US & Canada) and Random House Group Ltd. (UK & Rest of the World).

Inner Chapters by Chuang Tsu, trans. Gia-Fu Feng & Jane English, Wildwood House, with permission from Jane English.

Recommended Books and Websites

James Austin: *Zen and the Brain* (Cambridge, Mass: MIT Press. 1998)

Larry Culliford (as Patrick Whiteside): *The Little Book of Happiness* (London: Rider Books. 1998)

———— *The Little Book of Bliss* (London: Rider Books. 2000); *Happiness: The 30 day Guide* (London: Rider Books. 2001) For more details see: www.happinesssite.com

Neil Douglas-Klotz: *The Hidden Gospel: decoding the spiritual message of the Aramaic Jesus* (Wheaton, Illinois: Quest Books. 1999

Erik Erikson: *Identity and the Life Cycle* (New York: WW Norton. 1980)

————*The Life Cycle Completed* (New York: WW Norton. 1985)

William Faulkner:*Barn Burning* in *Faulkner's County* (London: Chatto & Windus. 1955); also available in

———— *Selected Short Stories of William Faulkner* (New York: Modern Library. 1993)

James Fowler:*Stages of Faith: the psychology of human development and the quest for meaning* (San Francisco: HarperSanFrancisco. 1981)

Viktor E. Frankl: *Man's Search for Meaning* (London: Rider Books. 1959, 2004)

Thich Nhat Hanh: *The Miracle of Mindfulness: a manual on*

meditation (London, Rider Books. 1975)

———— *Peace is Every Step: the path of mindfulness in every day life* (London, Rider Books. 1991)

Marie de Hennezel: *Intimate Death: how the dying teach us to live,* trans. Carol Brown Janeway (New York: Vintage Books. 1998)

Eugen Herrigel: *Zen in the Art of Archery* (London: Arkana. 1985)

———— *The Method of Zen* trans. R.F.C. Hull (London: Arkana 1988)

Harold Koenig, Michael McCullough & David Larson: *The Handbook of Religion and Health* (Oxford: Oxford University Press. 2001)

Thomas Merton: *Love and Living* (San Diego: Harcourt Inc. 1979)

———— *New Seeds of Contemplation* (New York: New Directions. 1961)

Dean Radin: *The Conscious Universe: the scientific truth of psychic phenomena* (San Francisco: HarperEdge. 1997)

Martin Rees: *Just Six Numbers: deep forces that shape the universe* (London: Phoenix. 1999)

Gail Sheehy: *Passages: Predictable Crises of Adult Life* (New York: Bantam.1977)

David Tacey: *The Spirituality Revolution* (Hove: Brunner-Routledge. 2004)

Chuang Tsu: *Inner Chapters* trans. Gia-Fu Feng and Jane English (London: Wildwood House. 1974)

Katsuki Sekida: *Zen Training: Methods and Philosophy* (New York: Weatherhill. 1975)

Mother Teresa: *A Simple Path* (New York: Ballantine Books.1995)

Evelyn Underhill:*The Spiritual Life: great spiritual truths for everyday life* (Oxford: Oneworld. 1993)

The Upanishads trans. Juan Mascaro (London: Penguin Books. 1965)

Alcoholics Anonymous www.alcoholics-anonymous.org

Bliss CDs www.blissfulmusic.com

Nikki Slade's music at www.freetheinnervoice.com

Royal College of Psychiatrists 'Spirituality and Psychiatry' Special Interest Group www.rcpsych.ac.uk/spirit

International Thomas Merton Society www.merton.org

Thomas Merton Society of Great Britain and Ireland www.thomasmertonsociety.org

Scientific and Medical Network www.scimednet.org

Multi Faith Group for Healthcare Chaplaincy www.mfghc.com

The Brahma Kumaris World Spiritual University www.bkwsu.org

The Janki Foundation for Global Health Care www.jankifoundation.org

O

is a symbol of the world,
of oneness and unity. O Books
explores the many paths of wholeness
and spiritual understanding which
different traditions have developed down
the ages. It aims to bring this knowledge
in accessible form, to a general readership,
providing practical spirituality to today's seekers.

For the full list of over 200 titles covering:

- CHILDREN'S PRAYER, NOVELTY AND GIFT BOOKS
- CHILDREN'S CHRISTIAN AND SPIRITUALITY
- CHRISTMAS AND EASTER
- RELIGION/PHILOSOPHY
- SCHOOL TITLES
- ANGELS/CHANNELLING
- HEALING/MEDITATION
- SELF-HELP/RELATIONSHIPS
- ASTROLOGY/NUMEROLOGY
- SPIRITUAL ENQUIRY
- CHRISTIANITY, EVANGELICAL
AND LIBERAL/RADICAL
- CURRENT AFFAIRS
- HISTORY/BIOGRAPHY
- INSPIRATIONAL/DEVOTIONAL
- WORLD RELIGIONS/INTERFAITH
- BIOGRAPHY AND FICTION
- BIBLE AND REFERENCE
- SCIENCE/PSYCHOLOGY

Please visit our website,
www.O-books.net

Don't Get MAD Get Wise
Why no one ever makes you angry, ever!
Mike George

There is a journey we all need to make, from anger, to peace, to forgiveness. Anger always destroys, peace always restores, and forgiveness always heals. This little book explains the journey, the steps you can take to make it happen for you.
1905047827 160pp £7.99 $14.95

Developing Spiritual Intelligence
The power of you
Altazar Rossiter

This beautifully clear and fascinating book is an incredibly simple guide to that which so many of us search for: the kind of spiritual intelligence that will enable us to live peacefully, intelligently, and joyfully whatever our circumstances. It brings the spiritual world down to earth, which is just where we need it to be in order to take our next step. Dr Dina Glouberman author of Life Choices, Life Changes and co-founder of Skyros
1905047649 240pp £12.99 $19.95

The 9 Dimensions of the Soul
Essence and the Enneagram
David Hey

The first book to relate the two, understanding the personality types of the Enneagram in relation to the Essence. In doing so it sheds a new light on our personality, its origins and how it operates, presenting an accurate map of our inner and outer self, our person-

ality and our inner being. The Nine Dimensions of the Soul is written in a beautifully simple, insightful and heartful way and transmits complex material in a way that is easy to read and understand. Thomas O. Trobe, MD Psychiatrist and Founder and Director of Learning Love Seminars, Inc.
1846940028 160pp £10.99 $19.95

Soul Power
The transformation that happens when you know
Nikki de Carteret
4th printing
This may be one of the finest books in its genre today. Using scenes from her own life and growth, Nikki de Carteret weaves wisdom about soul growth and the power of love and transcendent wisdom gleaned from the writings of the mystics. This is a book that I will read gain and again as a reference for my own soul growth. She is a scholar who is totally accessible and grounded in the human experience. Barnes and Noble review
190381636X 240pp £9.99 $15.95

Happiness in 10 Minutes
Brian Mountford
Brian Mountford-in exploring "happiness"-celebrates the paradox of losing and finding at its heart. At once both profound and simple, the book teaches us that to be fully alive is to be in communion and that gratitude leads us into the mystery of giving ourselves away-the path of true joy. Alan Jones, Dean of Grace Cathedral, San Francisco, author of Reimagining Christianity.
1905047770 128pp b/w illustrations £6.99 $9.95